SETTING THE RECORD STRAIGHT
THE WORD OF WISDOM

SETTING THE RECORD STRAIGHT

THE WORD
OF WISDOM

Steven C. Harper

Millennial Press, Inc.
P.O. Box 1741
Orem, UT 84059

ISBN: 1-932597-43-3

Cover design and typesetting by Adam Riggs

Dedication

To the memory of Paul Peterson, scholar and practitioner of the Word of Wisdom

Contents

Acknowledgments

This book is my best effort to teach the Word of Wisdom accurately and thoroughly. I acknowledge that there may be errors of fact or interpretation. If so, they are mine. I wrote the book at the invitation of Randy and Ryan Bott, whom I thank for the opportunity. Paul Peterson, the foremost scholar of the Word of Wisdom, would have written it under different circumstances. He was my kind and selfless friend who opened his research files to me. I depended very much on his work in preparing this book, and my greatest desire concerning it is that it reflect well on his legacy as a generous scholar. I am indebted to several other scholars as well, including especially Thomas Alexander. I am thankful to Heather Shumway for gathering and arranging the materials on which this book depends. Carolyn and John Harper taught me the Word of Wisdom by example and precept. My children—Hannah, John, Abigail, Seth, and Thomas—inspire me with good reasons to live it. Four-year-old Seth, for instance, prays every day that Heavenly Father will help him obey the Word of Wisdom. I offer the same prayer for myself and each of them. Jennifer Elizabeth has encouraged my work on this book and everything else worthwhile. I remain deeply thankful for her sustaining support.

A Chronology of the Word of Wisdom

Note: Bold typeface denotes events in LDS Church history.

c. 6000 BC

Tobacco begins growing in the Americas.

c.1 BC

Native Americans begin using tobacco in a number of ways.

470–630 AD

Tobacco use spreads through the Americas.

600–1000 AD

Pre-eleventh-century pottery found in Guatemala depicts a Maya smoking a roll of tobacco leaves.

1492

October 12, Columbus discovers America and tobacco.

Spaniards Roderigo de Perez and Luis de Torres search for China in Cuba. They observe natives lighting one end of a tobacco roll and "drinking" the smoke through the other. Perez acquires the habit and is thought to be the first smoker outside of the Americas.

1493

Ramon Pane, a monk on Columbus's second voyage, describes inhaling tobacco powder—snuff. Considered the first man to introduce tobacco to Europe.

1497

First written report of tobacco use appears in Europe; use of tobacco spreads.

1501

Roderigo de Perez is imprisoned by the Inquisition for smoking. Smoking becomes widespread in Spain before he is released years later.

1530

Early cigars become popular with Spanish lower classes.

1531

Europeans begin cultivating tobacco.

1556

Tobacco introduced to France.

1558

Tobacco introduced to Portugal.

1560–1

Frenchman Jean Nicot de Villemain celebrates tobacco's medicinal properties, describing it as a panacea; prescribes snuff to Queen Catherine de Medici for her son's migraine headaches.

1564–65

Tobacco introduced to mainstream English society.

1570s

Europeans laud the medicinal uses of tobacco.

1575

Roman Catholic Church forbids smoking in any place of worship in the Spanish Colonies.

1586

Virginia governor teaches Sir Walter Raleigh to smoke long-stemmed clay pipe.

German reports first to caution against tobacco use, calling it a "violent herb."

1590

First allusion to tobacco use in poetry.

1592–98

Japanese, who have learned of tobacco from Portuguese merchants, introduce tobacco to Korea.

1600

Sir Walter Raleigh persuades England's Queen Elizabeth to try smoking. "Everyone is doing it."

1601

Smoking denounced by Turkish clerics: "Puffing in each other's faces, they made the streets and markets stink," writes Ibrahim Pecevi.

c. 1601

Samuel Rowlands writes,
But this same poyson, steeped India weede
In head, hart, lunges, do the soote and cobwebs breede
With that he gasp'd, and breath'd out such a smoke
That all the standers by were like to choke.

1602–3

English writers debate tobacco use, appeal to King James.

1604

King James I of England publishes "A Counterblaste to Tobacco," increases taxes on imported tobacco by 4,000 percent.

1610

Sir Francis Bacon notes that tobacco use is rising and that the habit is hard to stop; her English writers publish recipes for tobacco's medicinal qualities but condemn casual use.

First tobacco vending machine.

1612

China forbids planting or using tobacco; Jamestown, Virginia produces first commercial crop.

1613–89

Russian Czars prohibit tobacco use.

1614

Spain's King Philip III establishes Seville as tobacco center of the world; cigarette use begins to spread.

1617

Dr. William Vaughn writes,
Tobacco that outlandish weede
It spends the braine and spoiles the seede
It dulls the spirite, it dims the sight
It robs a woman of her right.

Mongolian emperor imposes capital punishment for tobacco use.

1619

First Africans brought to Virginia to cultivate tobacco.

1620s

Tobacco use becomes Korean national pastime.

1642

Roman Catholic Pope issues statement against smoking in the churches in Seville.

1643

Russian Tsar declares smoking a deadly sin and orders smokers arrested and flogged or worse.

1647

Turkey lifts ban on "tobacck"; historian Pecevi writes that tobacco has joined coffee, wine, and opium as one of the four "cushions on the sofa of pleasure."

Connecticut bans public smoking.

1650

Connecticut forbids smoking by persons younger than 21.

1657

Switzerland prohibits smoking.

1665

An experiment at England's Royal Society leads to the death of a cat fed "a drop of distilled oil of tobacco."

1701

Scientist warns that young people taking too much tobacco have trembling, unsteady hands, staggering feet, and suffer a withering of "their noble parts."

1719

Smoking prohibited in France with some areas exempt.

1724

Roman Catholic Pope Benedict XIII learns to smoke and use snuff, repeals earlier papal statements against smoking by Catholic priests.

1730

First American tobacco factories begun in Virginia.

1758

Royal Factory of Seville begins and becomes world's largest tobacco processing factory until the 1950s.

1760

Pierre Lorillard establishes a "manufactory" in New York City for processing tobacco.

1761

Physician John Hill publishes what is probably the first clinical study of tobacco effects; warns snuff users they are vulnerable to cancers of the nose.

1773

John Wesley, founder of Methodism, denounces distilling alcoholic beverages as sinful and calls for its prohibition.

1779

Roman Catholic Pope Benedict XII opens a tobacco factory.

1785

American doctor Benjamin Rush publishes his *Inquiry into the Effects of Ardent Spirits Upon the Human Body and Mind.*

1787

Percival Pott connects snuff to cancer of the lip.

1790s

Lorillard creates the U.S.'s first national tobacco ad campaign.

1794

U.S. Congress passes the first federal excise tax on tobacco products.

1795

Samuel Thomas von Soemmering of Maine reports on cancers of the lip in pipe smokers.

1798

American physician Benjamin Rush writes on the medical dangers of tobacco and claims that smoking or chewing tobacco leads to drunkenness.

1805

Temperance movement gains momentum; Joseph Smith born in Vermont.

1805–7

Nicotine identified as the "essence" of tobacco.

1820

Joseph Smith envisions Heavenly Father and Jesus Christ near Manchester, New York.

1823

C. Clement Moore's 1823 poem "A Visit From St. Nicholas" describes Santa Claus as a pipe smoker.

1826

Organization of the American Temperance Society (later American Temperance Union) formed.

1828

Cigarettes become popular new way of smoking.

German scientists isolate nicotine in a pure form and conclude it is a "dangerous poison."

1830

April 6, Joseph Smith organizes restored Church of Jesus Christ, later known as The Church of Jesus Christ of Latter-day Saints.

1830s

First organized anti-tobacco movement in U.S. begins.

1832

Invention of the modern, paper-rolled cigarette.

Revelation to Joseph Smith called for establishment of a school for Mormon leaders known as the School of the Prophets (D&C 88).

1833

February 27, Joseph Smith receives a revelation known as the Word of Wisdom at a meeting of the school.

Georgia passes temperance law allowing counties to regulate alcohol.

1834

Joseph Smith Sr expresses gratitude to his son Hyrum for supporting him through past bouts of drunkenness.

Church council decision in Kirtland, Ohio, leads to enduring policy that Latter-day Saints who know the Word of Wisdom and choose not to obey it are not denied fellowship but generally are not called to official positions in the Church.

1835

Word of Wisdom published as section 80 in first edition of the Doctrine and Covenants.

1837

Seventies quorum in Kirtland, Ohio, enforces Word of Wisdom among its members.

1841

Joseph Smith tells Saints in Nauvoo, Illinois, that he is tempted by whiskey; says he "could live on it and get fat and feel well if God did not say it was sinful."

1842

Hyrum Smith gives landmark sermon on Word of Wisdom in Nauvoo, Illinois (see appendix A);
British writer Charles Dickens describes U.S. Congress as "the head-quarters of tobacco-tinctured saliva."

1843

Molecular composition of nicotine is established.

1847

Philip Morris begins selling Turkish cigarettes; Maine prohibits the sale of alcohol except for medicinal purposes.

1849

Tobacco company J.E. Liggett and Brother is established in St. Louis, Missouri.

Speaking of his observations among California gold rushers, one writer declares, "I have seen purer liquors, better seegars, finer tobacco, truer guns and pistols, larger dirks and bowie knives, and prettier cortezans, here in San Francisco than in any place I have ever visited, and it is my unbiased opinion that California can and does furnish the best bad things that are obtainable in America."

1849–51

Irish priest tours U.S., administers pledge of total abstinence from alcohol to some 600,000 persons in 25 states.

1851

Brigham Young asks Saints in Utah to renew their commitment to the Word of Wisdom.

1854

Philip Morris begins marketing his own cigarettes.

1855

"Annual Report of the New York Anti-Tobacco Society for 1855" calls tobacco a "fashionable poison," warns against addiction, and claims half of all deaths of smokers between the ages of 35 and 50 were caused by smoking.

1860

Mass manufacturing of cigarettes begins. Popular early brand, *Bull Durham*, becomes world famous and gives the term "bull pen" to baseball.

Lorillard wraps $100 bills at random in packages of cigarette tobacco named "Century," in order to celebrate the hundredth anniversary of the firm.

1860

Brigham Young gives up tobacco, alcohol, coffee, and tea for good.

1861

Brigham Young gives one of many sermons on temporal and spiritual importance of obeying the Word of Wisdom; this one is especially funny (see appendix B).

1864

1st American cigarette factory opens and produces almost twenty million cigarettes.

1869

National Prohibition Party formed in Chicago to work for prohibition of alcohol.

1871

Smoking banned on floor of U.S. House of Representatives; R.A. Patterson founds the "Lucky Strike" company in memory of the 1849 California Gold Rush.

Federal income tax is repealed, replaced by liquor and tobacco taxes to finance the federal budget.

1873

Formation of the Women's Christian Temperance Union.

1875

R.J. Reynolds founds R.J. Reynolds Tobacco Company.

1878

J.E. Liggett and Brother incorporates as Liggett & Myers Company.

1880s

Women's Christian Temperance Movement publishes a "Leaflet for Mothers' Meetings" titled "Narcotics," by Lida B. Ingalls. Discusses evils of tobacco, especially cigarettes. Cigarettes are "doing more to-day to undermine the constitution of our young men and boys than any other one evil."

1889

Scientists publish findings on nicotine damage to nerves; Buck Duke spends $800,000 in billboard and newspaper advertising.

Five leading cigarette firms unite to become American Tobacco Company.

1893

Evangelical Christians found Anti-Saloon League at Oberlin, Ohio, and lead the campaign for prohibition of alcohol.

1895

First known motion picture commercial is made, an ad for Admiral cigarettes.

1898

President Wilford Woodruff declares the "Word of Wisdom in its entirety as given of the Lord for the Latter-day Saints to observe, but he did not think that Bishops should withhold recommends from persons who did not adhere strictly to it."

1899

Lucy Payne Gaston, who claims that young men who smoke develop a distinguishable "cigarette face," founds the Chicago Anti-Cigarette League, which grows into a national, and then international, league to combat cigarette use.

First edition of the Merck Manual is published, recommending smoking to treat bronchitis and asthma.

1901

Cigarettes regulated in 43 of 45 states (Wyoming and Louisiana excepted); 3.5 billion cigarettes and 6 billion cigars are sold. Four in five American men smoke at least one cigar a day.

1905

In exchange for voting for the Food and Drug Act of 1906, tobacco state congressmen arrange for "tobacco" to be removed from the U.S. Pharmacopoeia, an official government listing of drugs, effectively removing tobacco from the list of substances regulated by the Food and Drug Administration.

President Joseph F. Smith urges stake presidents and bishops to be lenient toward elderly Saints who used coffee, tea, or tobacco, but to refuse temple recommends to Saints who flagrantly violated the Word of Wisdom.

1911

May 29, U.S. Supreme Court dissolves Duke's trust as a monopoly and in violation of the Sherman Anti-Trust Act (1890). Divisions of Duke become American Tobacco Co., R.J. Reynolds, Liggett & Myers Tobacco Company (Durham, NC), Lorillard, and British-American Tobacco.

1915

President Joseph F. Smith declares that middle-age men "who have experience in the Church should not be ordained to the Priesthood nor recommended to the privileges of the House of the Lord unless they will abstain from the use of tobacco and intoxicating drinks."

1917

Article by Frederick Pack in the Church's *Improvement Era* posed the question, "Should LDS Drink Coca-Cola?" Church leaders do not take official position.

1919

Ratification of the 18th Amendment prohibits the manufacture or sale of alcoholic beverages; Evangelist Billy Sunday declares "Prohibition is won; now for tobacco."

1920

Atlantic Monthly says, "scientific truth" has found "that the claims of those who inveigh against tobacco are wholly without foundation has been proved time and again by famous chemists, physicians, toxicologists, physiologists, and experts of every nation and clime."

1924

73 billion cigarettes sold in U.S.

1933

Congress adopts 21st Amendment to the Constitution, repealing earlier amendment prohibiting the manufacture and sale of alcohol.

Church's handbook of instructions for stake presidents and bishops explicitly says that Saints desiring to attend the temple "should keep the Word of Wisdom."

1940

Cigarette consumption grows by 2½ times since 1930; Adult Americans smoke 2,558 cigarettes per capita a year.

Journal of the American Medical Association publishes an article linking smoking with a higher risk of heart disease.

1950

Three epidemiological studies establish the link between smoking and lung cancer.

1953

Dr. Ernst L. Wynder establishes definitive biological link between smoking and cancer; tobacco consumption begins to decline; December 14, tobacco company executives meet at Plaza Hotel in New York City to find a way to deal with recent scientific data pointing to the health hazards of cigarettes. Results in hiring public relations firm Hill and Knowlton.

1957

Contrary to increased tobacco company advertising, the surgeon general declares link between smoking and lung cancer. "It is clear that there is an increasing and consistent body of evidence that excessive cigarette smoking is one of the causative factors in lung cancer." This is the first time a Public Health Service takes a position on tobacco smoking.

Readers Digest article reveals that tar and nicotine levels in so-called "filtered" cigarettes have risen steadily to nearly the same levels as unfiltered brands.

1960s

Tobacco companies win litigation against them; surgeon general begins issuing annual reports on the health consequences of smoking.

1962

Amidst increasingly strident debate between scientists and tobacco companies, advertisers and anti-tobacco activists, comedian Bob Newhart satirizes "The Introduction of Tobacco to Civilization."

1963

Trying to emphasize its healthful properties, Tobacco company lawyer acknowledges in a memo that "nicotine is addictive. We are, then, in the business of selling nicotine, an addictive drug effective in the release of stress mechanisms."

1964

American Medical Association accepts $10 million grant from tobacco companies for research. The AMA postpones plans to report on smoking's relationship to cancer; instead it supports tobacco industry's objection to labeling cigarettes as a health hazard.

1971

Cigarette ads no longer air on American television and radio.

1970s

Tobacco company documents reveal conspiracy to regulate nicotine levels and market tobacco to youth. One tobacco company research scientist writes, "Happily for the tobacco industry, nicotine is both habituating and unique in its variety of physiological actions, hence no other active material or combination of materials provides equivalent 'satisfaction.'"

1984

Federal regulation of tobacco marketing becomes stricter.

1987

Joe Camel debuts as tobacco advertising icon; former "Marlboro Man" ad icon David Millar Jr. dies of emphysema.

1988

President Gordon B. Hinckley responds to excuse that illicit drugs are not forbidden by Word of Wisdom: "What a miserable excuse. There is likewise no mention of the hazards of diving into an empty swimming pool or of jumping from an overpass onto the freeway. But who doubts the deadly consequences of such? Common sense would dictate against such behavior."

1990

San Luis Obispo, California, first city in the world to ban smoking in all public buildings.

1991

Journal of the American Medical Association publishes studies of Joe Camel's powerful influence on preschoolers and under-18 smokers.

1992

Cigarette ad model Will Thornbury dies of lung cancer at age of 56.

1994

Largest ever class action lawsuit charges that tobacco companies hid their knowledge of the addicting qualities of tobacco. Mississippi becomes first state to sue tobacco companies to recover health care costs incurred by smoking. Case filed by Mississippi Attorney General Michael Moore, who shares his "conspiracy theory" with LDS general authorities in 1997.

2000

U.S. smoking consumption down nearly 50 percent since 1976; China has 385 million smokers.

What is the Word of Wisdom?

Perhaps you have heard of the Word of Wisdom from friends, parents, or a Sunday school teacher, with the assumption that you would know what they were talking about. This book is for anyone who has wondered, what in the world is the Word of Wisdom? Or who would like to gain a better understanding of what it is, how it came to be, how it has been understood and applied historically, and what it means to Latter-day Saints today.

The Word of Wisdom is a revelation from God to Joseph Smith. In 1820, Joseph Smith was a religiously frustrated teenager in western New York who acted on the Bible's promise that "if any of you lack wisdom, let him ask of God, that giveth to all men liberally . . . and it shall be given him" (James 1:5). Joseph said that his prayer was answered by two heavenly beings, God and Jesus Christ, who descended from heaven and taught him that the existing Christian churches had become corrupted. The churches were so dependent on written creeds that they rejected the power of God, claiming that he no longer gave revelation to mankind on earth. God bypassed such "professors" of religion and chose Joseph to restore the church Christ had originally established. Latter-day Saints believe, then, in the restoration of true Christianity. They reject the creeds that developed to define God and Christ, and they reject the idea that God ceased to give revelation sometime in the past.

Joseph Smith restored the Church of Christ in 1830. It later became known as The Church of Jesus Christ of Latter-day Saints, and from the beginning was referred to as "Mormon" because Joseph translated and published the Book of Mormon as additional scripture to testify that salvation comes by faith in and obedience to Jesus Christ.

Three years after publishing the Book of Mormon and restoring the Church, Joseph Smith received one of his many revelations. It was first written into a manuscript book with other revelations, and then published as a single sheet at the end of 1833. In 1835, it was published as section 80 of the first edition of the Doctrine and Covenants. Today it is best known as section 89 of the Doctrine and Covenants. What does the revelation say? Even long-time believers may give poor answers to this question. The revelation is readily available but seldom studied seriously. As a result, it is often understood superficially even by people who believe in its divinity.

The revelation is introduced as a word of wisdom to benefit the high priests and general church members in Kirtland, Ohio, where Joseph Smith lived, and in Independence, Missouri, which the Lord had designated as Zion, a gathering place for Latter-day Saints anticipating the second coming of Jesus Christ. The revelation said it was to be sent to these believers not as a commandment, but as a revelation of wisdom, showing the will of God for the temporal salvation of all Latter-day Saints, given with a promise and adapted to the weakest saint. The Lord gave this wisdom to warn against conspiracies that do and will exist. He forbade drinking strong drinks and also wine, unless it was for the sacrament or eucharist, in which case it should be pure wine the Saints make themselves. Strong drinks are for washing the body. Tobacco is not to be ingested, but used with judgment and skill in treating bruises and sick cattle. Hot drinks are not to be ingested either. God made wholesome herbs for human consumption, each in season, to be used with "prudence and thanksgiving." God created animals and birds to be used thankfully and sparingly by mankind. It displeases him if such are used unless circumstances of winter, cold, or famine dictate. God ordained all grains to be the staff of life for man, domesticated animals, fowls, and wild animals. Wild animals he made for mankind to use in times of excessive hunger. All grain, fruits, and vegetables are good food for mankind, particularly wheat for man, corn for oxen, oats for horses, rye for fowls and pigs and other domesticated animals. Barley and other grains are good for useful animals generally, and for mild drinks. All Saints who remember to keep and do the behaviors outlined in this revelation receive health, wisdom, and "great treasures of knowledge" as a result. They can run and not be weary, walk and not faint. The Lord promises them protection from the destroying angel from which he preserved the Israelites.[1]

There is much more going on in the revelation than the usual way it gets boiled down as a ban on alcohol, tobacco, coffee, and tea. One of the first things to notice is the doctrinal basis for the revelation. It assumes, as an earlier revelation to Joseph Smith said, that "the spirit and the body are the soul of man" (D&C 88:15). Whereas some Christians think of the body as evil and look forward to leaving it behind at death, Latter-day Saints regard the body as godly and look forward to a literal, glorious resurrection. They believe God and Christ are perfectly embodied and that through the process of birth, earth-life, death, and resurrection, men and women are being created in their image. For these reasons, practical wisdom on the care of the body is no less religious to Latter-day Saints than is prayer.[2]

1. Gordon B. Hinckley, "Excerpts from Recent Addresses of President Gordon B. Hinckley," *Ensign,* July 1996, 72–73.
2. Joseph Fielding Smith, comp., *Teachings of the Prophet Joseph Smith* (Salt Lake City: Deseret Book, 1976), 181.

The Word of Wisdom rests on three other important doctrines, namely agency, stewardship, and accountability. These doctrines are everywhere in the revelations to Joseph Smith. Agency is the power to act independently. Stewardship is what one has to act on. Accountability is the end result. Every agent ultimately accounts to God for what they did with the stewardship he gave them. The Word of Wisdom assumes that mankind has agency. Not all Christians believe that God has given mankind this power. Joseph Smith's ancestors did not. His revelations demonstrated that God had given this wonderful power to act, to choose, to mankind. This agency needs to be understood. It is not freedom from making choices; it is the freedom and power to make choices. A free agent must act. They have to choose. And there are inevitable consequences for each choice. You can see agency in the revelation as God declares his will. By communicating this knowledge, God makes us free to act. Some think that revelations, commandments, and laws curtail freedom, but that is not so. Knowing God's will does not coerce anyone to do it. Knowing God's will enables a person to knowingly, of their own free will, obey or disobey it. Not knowing God's will means the person remains ignorant and can't act in ways that please God except by accident, not by free will. Thus there is no agency until one knows God's will. Notice that the Word of Wisdom declares God's will for the temporal or bodily salvation of all Saints in the last days. It is adapted to the weakest saint, and thus not beyond the power of anyone to obey or disobey as they please. It is not God determining destinies, but rather God giving agency by giving knowledge and thus the power to choose.

One's stewardship is what one has to act on. The most notable stewardship in the Word of Wisdom is one's own body, but there are several others. The revelation instructs how to act relative to distilled and fermented beverages, domesticated and wild animals, tobacco, hot drinks, and all kinds of grain, herbs, fruits, and vegetables. These are all things God has made and given mankind to use. The revelation tells mankind how to use them in ways that please God. "All these to be used with prudence and thanksgiving," for example, speaking of herbs and fruits (D&C 89:11), or "they are to be used sparingly," speaking of meat and poultry (D&C 89:12). A seldom noted aspect of stewardship in the Word of Wisdom is the repeated command to use what God has provided "with thanksgiving" (D&C 89:11–12). In the Word of Wisdom, God is clearly the owner. Evidence is seen in phrases like "all wholesome herbs God hath ordained for the constitution, nature, and *use* of man" or "flesh also of beasts and of the fowls of the air, I, the Lord, have ordained for the *use* of man," or "and these God hath made for the *use* of man" (D&C 89:10, 12, 15; emphasis added). The repeated emphasis is on *use*, not *abuse*. God created this earth and its life-sustaining abundance to be used by wise stewards who thankfully acknowledge him, not abused by the ungrateful or gluttonous.

The doctrine of accountability is also evident in the Word of Wisdom. Good stewards recognize that they are not the owner of the stewardship, but that they are accountable to the owner for the way they act in regard to what the owner provides. The last four verses of the revelation describe the promised blessings granted to those who act wisely on the stewardship God has provided. Note the powerful verbs: "Those who *remember* to *keep* and *do* these sayings, *walking* in obedience to the commandments, shall receive health in their navel and marrow to their bones; And shall find wisdom and great treasures of knowledge, even hidden treasures; And shall run and not be weary, and shall walk and not faint. And I, the Lord give unto them a promise, that the destroying angel shall pass by them, as the children of Israel, and not slay them" (D&C

89:18–21; emphasis added). The promise of preservation from death or the destroying angel is conditional. It is guaranteed to those who remember, keep, do, and walk in obedience to the commandments in the Word of Wisdom. No one has to remember, keep, do, or obey those commandments. The commands themselves make us free to obey or disobey of our own free will. But no one escapes accountability for the way they act, and only those who choose to act wisely can expect the promised wisdom, knowledge, health, and deliverance.

Summed up, the doctrines of agency, stewardship, and accountability make the Word of Wisdom a "principle with promise," as it calls itself (D&C 89:3). It is an if/then contract. If (the principle) Saints choose to obey God's will as described in the revelation, then (the promise) he preserves their lives and endows them with wisdom. This is not the fountain of youth. It is not quick or easy or available for three easy installments of $29.99. It is not a guarantee that you'll look like you just came from the plastic surgeon, or that you will lose thirty pounds in thirty days, or have perfect abs with just five minutes a day, or never get wrinkles. It is not a promise that you will not die. It is a very specific principle with a very specific promise: those who obey all the commands in the revelation can expect to be delivered from death "as the children of Israel" (D&C 89:21).

How were the children of Israel delivered? Moses revealed God's very specific instructions to the elders of the Israelites enslaved in Egypt. They were to take a lamb and kill it, dip a handful of twigs and leaves in the blood, and smear the blood above and beside the doors of their homes, and then stay inside the door until morning. The Lord would not allow the destroyer to enter such houses. While the firstborn among the Egyptians were smitten, obedient Israelites were delivered from death and then from slavery (Exodus 12). The Word of Wisdom was revealed to Joseph Smith by the same Lord who spoke to Moses. The Savior's redeeming blood, signified by the blood of the Passover lamb, saves all mankind, not arbitrarily as Joseph Smith's ancestors believed, but because free agents choose to be saved by obeying the terms and conditions on which the Lord predicates his saving grace. He communicates his will to mankind through prophets like Moses and Joseph Smith. These revelations have the powerful effect of giving us wisdom and knowledge, which enables us to act for ourselves in ways that deliver us from all kinds of bondage and lead to salvation both temporal and eternal.

The Word of Wisdom is much, much more than a list of thou shalt nots. It is more than a simple health code. It is a covenant. Elder Boyd K. Packer testified that "while the Word of Wisdom requires strict obedience, in return it promises health, great treasures of knowledge, and that redemption bought for us by the Lamb of God, who was slain that we might be redeemed."[3]

---

3. Boyd K. Packer, "The Word of Wisdom: The Principle and the Promises," *Ensign*, May 1996, 18.

What Circumstances Led to the Word of Wisdom Being Given?

Revelations answer questions. The questions stem from the circumstances of the one asking them. To identify the origins of the Word of Wisdom, we must begin by asking what Joseph Smith's questions were, and, just as important, what were the circumstances that caused him to ask them?

Joseph Smith's mother said that he preferred his father's embrace more than liquor to numb the pain of a leg operation when he was seven years old, but neither Joseph or his family were strangers to alcohol. Most everyone drank in the 1820s and 1830s, Joseph Smith included.[4] Distillers in his upstate New York neighborhood made corn whiskey and sent 65,277 gallons of it and 69 tons of beer to market on the Erie Canal the year after Joseph's first vision of God and Christ.[5] Newspapers in the towns near Joseph's home advertised cheap alcohol, printed recipes for making beer, and local merchants sold the ingredients. One scholar called Joseph Smith's America "the alcoholic republic."[6] Joseph's father confessed in 1834 that he had in the past been "out of the way through wine," but "Joseph Sr.'s drinking was not excessive for that time and place."[7] Near-

4. *Saints Herald*, June 1, 1881, 163, 167.
5. *Western Farmer*, January 30, 1822.
6. W.J. Rorabaugh, *The Alcoholic Republic: An American Tradition* (New York: Oxford University Press, 1979).
7. Richard Lyman Bushman, *Joseph Smith: Rough Stone Rolling* (New York: Knopf, 2005), 42.

ly all males drank and many women and children. Members of all social classes drank. Elites drank expensive foreign wines; working-class folks drank ciders and whiskey, but almost all drank a lot. They drank morning, mid-day, and evening, at funerals and parties, militia musters and church socials. Drinking had a long and happy heritage in America. There were only a few outspoken opponents of alcohol consumption in the 1700s, but their warnings fell largely on deaf ears as consumption rates rose between 1790 and 1830.

Digital Image © 2003 Utah State Historical Society. All Rights Reserved.

Joseph Smith, Sr., was the father of first LDS Church President Joseph Smith.

America in the 1830s pulsed with evils and reformers determined to combat them. By the time Joseph Smith moved to Kirtland, Ohio, in 1831, more Americans were beginning to become concerned with social vices generally and alcohol abuse especially. Besides slavery, gambling, and political corruption, debate swirled about the appropriate use of alcohol. Reformers advocated temperance, or the moderate use of alcohol. "The thing has arrived to such a height," one widely-quoted temperance advocate noted, "that we are actually threatened with becoming a nation of drunkards."[8] Concerned citizens formed the American Temperance Society in 1826 and quickly organized two hundred and twenty-two local chapters in sixteen states.[9] Temperance advocates organized in Susquehanna County, Pennsylvania, in 1828—where Joseph Smith was translating the Book of Mormon. Shortly thereafter two

8. Quoted in Rorabaugh, *Alcoholic Republic*, 216.
9. Ernest H. Cherrington, *The Evolution of Prohibition in the United States of America* (Westerville, Ohio: American Issue Press, 1920), 93.

local distillers and several merchants stopped making and selling liquor.[10]

America's desire for alcohol and the rise of temperance generated diverse opinions that led Joseph Smith to ask questions. Some activists wanted total abstinence from alcohol. They condemned producers and sellers, and tried to get citizens to make temperance pledges, or promises to abstain. Others advocated temperate use. Between 1831 and 1836, the cry for abstinence gained momentum. In 1833, in the middle of this controversy, the Lord clarified in the Word of Wisdom where the Saints should stand relative to this controversy.

Christopher Columbus introduced Europe to tobacco after Native Americans introduced it to him. In Europe, tobacco gained a reputation as a miracle drug, and by the 1500s it was prescribed as a cure for cancer, gout, asthma (ironically), ulcers, arrow wounds, flatulence, toothaches, bad breath, warts, deafness, constipation, tonsillitis, nose bleeds, epilepsy, and a host of other afflictions. Smoking quickly caught on among European elites, though not all. King James of England considered smoking "loathsome to the eye, hateful to the nose, harmful to the brain, dangerous to the lungs," but the increasing demand for tobacco made it a cash crop in Virginia.[11] "Was Virginia to supplement England's economy and redeem her rogues by pandering to a new vice?" one historian asked. "The answer, of course, was yes."[12]

By the seventeenth century, elites were adopting a French practice of sniffing powdered tobacco—snuff—while smoking

10. Rick Grunder, Description of Temperance Collection, 1788–1848, citing *National Philanthropist and People's Advocate*, June 17, 1829, L. Tom Perry Special Collections, Harold B. Lee Library, Brigham Young University.

11. "A Counterblaste to Tobacco," by King James I of England, VI of Scotland, 1604.

12. Edmund S. Morgan, *American Slavery, American Freedom* (New York: Norton, 1975), 90–91.

had spread to working class folks. The Spanish smoked cigars. Americans chewed. Charles Dickens observed congressmen preparing a plug of chewing tobacco, then "when it is quite ready for use, shooting the old one from his mouth as from a pop-gun, and clapping the new one in its place."[13] A new method for delivering the powerfully addictive nicotine found in tobacco—the cigarette—was just about to spread across the globe when Joseph Smith received the Word of Wisdom in 1833. By mid-century, men named Philip Morris, J.E. Liggett, Washington Duke, and then R.J. Reynolds would begin the mass manufacture and marketing of tobacco, both generating and satisfying a massive addiction to nicotine.

Outspoken temperance crusaders added tobacco to their list of noxious substances in the 1830s. Many of the same stores that sold liquor also sold tobacco. Opponents of tobacco use regarded it as akin to liquor. One said that tobacco use created thirst only liquor could quench. Another called tobacco poison. Former U.S. President John Quincy Adams noted his youthful addiction to tobacco, adding, "I was warned by a medical friend of the pernicious operation of this habit upon the stomach and the nerves."[14]

Was tobacco a powerful medicine capable of curing all kinds of afflictions or a noxious weed that was loathsome to the lungs? Was it filthy habit or a socially acceptable pastime? Uncertainty about these questions may have been the immediate catalyst for Joseph Smith's reception of the Word of Wisdom. He organized classes for the Church's adult men in an upstairs room of Newel Whitney's store in Kirtland, Ohio. When the brethren gathered for class, according to Brigham Young, "the first thing they did was to light their pipes, and, while smoking,

---

13. Charles Dickens, *American Notes* (Konemann: Hungary, 2000).
14. J.Q. Adams to Reverend Samuel H. Cox, August 19, 1845, cited in Benjamin I. Lane, *The Mysteries of Tobacco* (New York: Wiley and Putnam, 1845), 32.

talk about the great things of the kingdom, and spit all over the room, and as soon as the pipe was out of their mouths a large chew of tobacco would then be taken. Often when the Prophet entered the room to give the school instructions he would find himself in a cloud of tobacco smoke. This, and the complaints of his wife at having to clean so filthy a floor, made the Prophet think upon the matter, and he inquired of the Lord relating to the conduct of the elders in using tobacco, and the revelation known as the Word of Wisdom was the result."[15]

There was no consensus of medical opinion in the nineteenth century. The prevailing medical theory held that diseases or disorders were caused by an imbalance in a person's inner energy source. Over-stimulation, it was thought, resulted in fevers or infections. Treatments aimed at releasing the excess energy through bleeding or purging or changing one's diet. Lethargic patients were thought to be lacking nervous energy, and were therefore treated with diets or medicines designed to stimulate. Coffee and tea were often used as stimulants by those struggling with a lack of energy. Some herbs, spices, and fruits served the same purpose, especially pepper and mustard. Medical professionals disagreed about how much of these substances could be safely consumed, and by whom. One author noted that "a pineapple or a watermelon" could effectively be "a death warrant."[16] Americans consumed enormous amounts of meat. Authorities often condoned this practice in winter but worried that too much consumption could result in over-stimulation. All authorities agreed that use of all stimulants, in which they included herbs, meats, coffee, and tea, could lead to over-stimulation and therefore disease. The most radical authorities, especially Sylvester Graham, thought that foods

15. Brigham Young, in *Journal of Discourses*, 26 vols. (Liverpool: F.D. Richards, 1855–86), 12:158, February 8, 1868.
16. Quoted in Lester E. Bush, Jr., "The Word of Wisdom in Early Nineteenth-Century Perspective," *Dialogue* 14, no. 3 (1981): 60.

much more tasty than a Graham cracker (named for Sylvester) were very dangerous. He urged complete abstinence from coffee, tea, meat, spices, and condiments. Granting that coffee and tea were stimulants, other authorities thought Graham's position too extreme and believed that healthy people could consume these drinks in moderation without causing disease.

By 1800, the influential doctor Benjamin Rush had persuaded many authorities that all disease could be traced to over-stimulation, and therefore all illness could be treated by so-called "heroic" methods of releasing the patient's excess energy. Joseph Smith's brother Alvin died in 1823 after a doctor's dose of mercurous chloride blocked rather than purged his digestive system. Joseph Smith and most Latter-day Saints had little confidence in the fledgling medical profession and its heroic practices. In the days of primitive diagnostic techniques before diseases were well understood, an 1831 revelation to Joseph Smith taught Saints that "whosoever among you are sick, and have not faith to be healed, but believe, shall be nourished with all tenderness, with herbs and mild food, and that not by the hand of an enemy" (D&C 42:43). This counsel matched most closely the relatively innocuous naturopathic practices of Samuel Thomson, and many Latter-day Saints followed his advice until advances in medical science increased their confidence in professionals late in the nineteenth century.[17]

The world into which the Lord revealed the Word of Wisdom was quite different from our own. Advances in medical science have provided much more certainty about the dangers of consuming many of the substances that were thought by many in Joseph Smith's world to have medicinal value. Moreover, his contemporaries were in the process of reconsidering their certainty about the value of alcohol, tobacco, coffee, tea,

17. Cecil O. Samuelson Jr., "Medical Practices," in *Encyclopedia of Mormonism*, ed. Daniel H. Ludlow, 4 vols. (New York: MacMillan, 1992), 2: 875.

meats, fruits, and some herbs. There was no prevailing view to which everyone subscribed, even inside the Church. There were more questions than answers.

Some critics of the Word of Wisdom assert that because it addressed the circumstances of Joseph Smith's world, it must not be real revelation. This logic is simplistic and flawed. Its first error is to assume that revelation that answers timely questions is somehow suspect. What good is an irrelevant revelation? We seek, and the Lord gives, revelations that answer the questions and problems of the day, and because those questions and problems change with circumstances, revelations to Moses or Peter are not always adequate for our needs. Another error critics make is the simplistic assumption that the Word of Wisdom mimicked the prevailing idea of Joseph's time. But there was no single opinion. Then as now there were many competing ideas, debate rather than consensus. The Word of Wisdom sorts out and clarifies the strengths and weaknesses among the variety of opinions.

How Did the Revelation Answer the Questions of the Day?

Nearly two dozen men gathered for school in a second-story room of Newel and Ann Whitney's Kirtland, Ohio, store on February 27, 1833. With one of them for his scribe and perhaps one or two others present, Joseph Smith, in a nearby room, received the revelation known as the Word of Wisdom. Besides answering the immediate question of whether the brethren should smoke or chew tobacco, or "the filthy weed and their disgusting slobbering and spitting" as one colorful account put it, the revelation clarified several other issues that were being debated by Joseph's contemporaries.[18]

One of the most contested issues of the early nineteenth century was whether alcohol consumption was appropriate, and if so, how much and by whom. The Word of Wisdom gave the Lord's will with regard to the various types of alcoholic beverages—distilled and fermented. Strong or distilled drinks like brandy or whiskey have the highest alcohol content. The revelation declared these were useful for washing the outside of the body, not the belly. Fermented drinks like wine and beer were not to be ingested, with the exception of wine the Saints made themselves for sacramental purposes and the possible exception of mildly fermented drinks made from barley and containing a negligible amount of alcohol. Familiar as they were with this range of beverages, Joseph Smith and his contemporaries knew

18. Lyndon W. Cook, ed., *David Whitmer Interviews* (Orem, Utah: Grandin, 1991), 204.

that not all alcoholic beverages were created equal. It is useful to learn enough about them to understand the Word of Wisdom.

Other questions of Joseph's Smith contemporaries, including followers and his family members, dealt with tobacco, coffee, and tea. The revelation acknowledged medicinal value in tobacco, but prescribed it for treating bruises and sick cattle. It was not to be ingested either by smoking, sniffing, or chewing. The revelation declared hot drinks unfit for ingestion. Soon thereafter Joseph Smith clarified that tea and coffee "are what the Lord meant when He said Hot drinks."[19] Speaking before the Saints in 1842, Hyrum Smith quoted the Word of Wisdom passage on hot drinks, then interpreted it as Joseph had a decade earlier: "I say it does refer to tea, and coffee."[20] Considerable evidence testifies that Saints in the 1830s understood hot drinks to include tea and coffee, and that they struggled to act on this wisdom.[21]

Other nineteenth-century debates concerned meats, herbs, fruits, and vegetables. By declaring that herbs and fruits should be used in season with prudence and thanksgiving, the Word of Wisdom approved the moderate position of the medical profession of the time. So did the revelation's declaration that meat eaten sparingly and especially in winter was healthful. These aspects of the revelation ran counter to the advice of extremists like Sylvester Graham, who had less in common with the Word of Wisdom than is sometimes assumed. As one medical scholar wrote, "the Word of Wisdom represents a response to more specific circumstances than we often assume today."[22]

19. Joel H. Johnson, *Voice From the Mountains* (Salt Lake City: Juvenile Instructor Office, 1881), 12.
20. Hyrum Smith, "The Word of Wisdom," *Times and Seasons*, June 1, 1842, 799–801.
21. Paul H. Peterson, "An Historical Analysis of the Word of Wisdom," (M.A. thesis, Brigham Young University, 1972), 22.
22. Bush, "The Word of Wisdom in Early Nineteenth-Century Perspective," 60.

In sum, the Word of Wisdom answered questions of the day in unpredictable ways. Forbidding the ingestion of nearly all alcoholic beverages as well as coffee, tea, and tobacco, the revelation ran counter to the mainstream culture. But it was also consistent with an emerging medical opinion regarding meats, herbs, fruits, and vegetables. The revelation did not give Joseph Smith, his followers, or family members what they wanted to hear. Nearly all the men in the school used tobacco. Joseph's wife Emma consumed coffee and tea. Joseph liked whiskey.[23] They all consumed more meat than was needful.[24] The revelation was not what they wanted to hear. It was the wisdom they needed to hear.

---

23. Joseph Smith address to the Mormons at Nauvoo on Last Sunday of April 1841, Reverend Julius A. Reed Collection, box 2, folder 15, Iowa State Historical Society, Iowa City, Iowa.
24. Bush, "The Word of Wisdom in Early Nineteenth-Century Perspective," 53, 63.

What Evils and Designs Exist in the Hearts of Conspiring Men?

It is clear that Joseph Smith sought the revelation because of the questions his circumstances generated. But the revelation itself does something far beyond answering questions then current. The Word of Wisdom states that it was given because "of evils and designs which do and will exist in the hearts of conspiring men in the last days" (D&C 89:4). It forewarns future Saints how to act wisely in the midst of conspiracies designed to harm them. It is hard to overstate how remarkably prophetic the revelation is. Joseph Smith knew of no conspiracies existing in the hearts of conspiring men in his day, to say nothing of ours. Yet some of those conspiracies have come to light in the last generation. Saints who wisely heeded the forewarning escaped the evil designs against them.

The health benefits of applying all aspects of the Word of Wisdom have become increasingly clear. Most obviously, tobacco was linked to lung cancer in the 1950s, and since then numerous other health problems have been linked to smoking, including heart disease and birth defects. Yet it was in the decades prior to these discoveries that the Word of Wisdom's forewarning could have blessed mankind most. World War I witnessed widespread cigarette smoking among men. World War II saw women begin smoking in large numbers. Tobacco marketers associated their products with patriotic duty. Manufacture and marketing of tobacco peaked after World War II, generating enormous profits as well as tax revenues for local, state, and national governments who, as a result, were (and in many cases remain) reluctant to regulate tobacco. Mounting scientific evidence brought governments slowly to increasingly regulate the marketing and manufacture of tobacco products, but tobacco companies have simply moved their efforts to vulnerable populations in countries that are not well-equipped to combat them. One tactic of the conspirators is to smuggle millions of cigarettes into such countries and then persuade national leaders that they are losing tax revenue, so why not legalize and then tax the cigarettes.[25] Tobacco companies purchase influence while causing a public health crisis that has become a global pandemic.[26]

Shortly after the scientific evidence linked cigarette smoking with lung cancer, fiercely competitive executives of America's largest tobacco companies met at the Plaza Hotel in New York City and became allies. They employed a public relations firm to sell the idea that public health was their most important concern. If cigarettes were as harmful as science indicated, their pitch declared, then obviously the tobacco companies would stop selling them. One non-Mormon analyst said that this "meeting marked the beginning of the conspiracy."[27]

In the 1960s, scientists began officially stating that smoking caused lung cancer. The tobacco conspiracy countered by organizing themselves and spending millions on advertising in what one professor called a "scheme to defraud" that differed

25. *The Tobacco Conspiracy*, DVD, directed by Nadia Collot (National Film Board of Canada and KUIV Productions, 2006); Richard Kluger, *Ashes to Ashes* (New York: Knopf, 1996).

26. Russell M. Nelson, "Addiction or Freedom," *Ensign*, November 1988, 6.

27. Richard D. Hurt and Channing R. Robertson, "Prying Open the Door to the Tobacco Industry's Secrets About Nicotine," *Journal of the American Medical Association* 280, no. 13 (1998): 1173–74. *The Tobacco Conspiracy*, DVD.

little from organized crime. They also sponsored what has been called "scientific subversion" by hiring scientists to produce findings consistent with tobacco company aims.[28]

A major part of the conspiracy has been to aggressively market tobacco to youth. Documents evidence that tobacco companies knew at least as early as 1975 that "nicotine is addictive," and that "we are in the business of selling an addictive drug." With that knowledge, marketing efforts have been aimed at children and youth. "It is important to know as much as possible about teenage smoking patterns and attitudes," a 1981 tobacco company document says. "Today's teenager is tomorrow's potential regular customer." Knowing, as another document says, that "positive images for cigarettes are created by cinema and television," conspirators used those media to attract young smokers. As one young woman put it, "once you're mature enough to say smoking's dumb, it's too late." The United States banned tobacco ads on television in 1971, but movies remain a powerful recruiting tool. Images of smoking movie stars declined between 1950 and 1990, but since then have risen higher than ever. Tobacco companies contract with the most popular movie stars to smoke on film. Perhaps viewers hardly notice, but the tobacco conspiracy notices and puts its money where it does the most damage.[29]

In 1997, the leaders of America's largest tobacco companies swore before a congressional hearing that they did not think nicotine was addictive. Their own documents proved otherwise. In 1998, the *Journal of the American Medical Association* reported that the tobacco industry had known for decades and had secretly acknowledged that nicotine was addictive, and that cigarettes were ideal instruments for delivering the drug. Even worse, tobacco company scientists, executives, and marketers conspired to manipulate nicotine levels and to target children

28. *The Tobacco Conspiracy*, DVD.
29. *The Tobacco Conspiracy*, DVD.

and youth in order to ensure a perpetual market for what they knew was poison.

Governments, paralyzed between promoting general welfare and raising revenue, struggle to act. And when they do the tobacco conspiracy finds new avenues of attack. The United States finally banned Joe Camel in the 1990s when evidence revealed that tobacco companies were successfully using the character to promote their products to children. Now tobacco company brands are conspicuous on clothing worn by children in Africa and elsewhere.

In the 1990s, with the evils and designs in the hearts of conspiring men clearly evident, several states filed suit against tobacco companies. In 1997, Mississippi Attorney General Michael Moore visited Salt Lake City, where he was hosted by general authorities of The Church of Jesus Christ of Latter-day Saints, W. Eugene Hansen and Marlin K. Jensen. All three men were lawyers, and their conversation turned naturally to the legal action Mississippi, Utah, and other states were then taking against tobacco companies. Moore explained that his legal strategy was to prove a "conspiracy" on the part of tobacco companies, using the overwhelming evidence that had come to light in the internal documents that revealed their intentions. Elder Jensen drew Moore's attention to the fourth verse of the Word of Wisdom. "We listened attentively," Elder Jensen said, "as he slowly and deliberately read that verse out loud in his appealing southern accent: 'Behold, verily, thus saith the Lord unto you: In consequence of evils and designs which do and will exist in the hearts of conspiring men in the last days, I have warned you, and forewarn you, by giving you this word of wisdom by revelation'" (D&C 89:4). Elder Jensen noted that "the scriptural reference to 'conspiring men' was not lost on Mr. Moore. As he finished reading verse 4, a broad smile came across his face, and with a twinkle in his eye he said, 'I never dreamed in visiting Utah I might find 10 million people who would agree with my conspiracy theories!'"[30]

Elder Jensen testified: "My heart burned within me that day and has many times since as I have thought about Joseph Smith's gift as a prophet and seer. There is really no other explanation for the origin of that 1833 revelation. It waited until nearly the end of the twentieth century for an almost literal verification of one of its key passages. In the hearts of the faithful Saints who have heeded its message for nearly 170 years, however, there has never been any doubt about its authenticity or relevance."[31]

---

30. Marlin K. Jensen, "May the Kingdom of God Go Forth," in *Out of Obscurity* (Salt Lake City: Deseret Book, 2000), 9–10.
31. Jensen, "May the Kingdom of God Go Forth," 9–10.

Did Joseph Smith Obey the Word of Wisdom?

Joseph Smith stood before the Saints in Nauvoo, Illinois, in April 1841 and, with good humor, said: "What are my temptations? Whiskey whiskey whiskey." He said he "could live on it and get fat and feel well if God did not say it was sinful. He would not wrestle with it," Joseph continued, "for he could not throw it."[32] Joseph made no secret of the fact that he enjoyed a glass of wine or even a shot of whiskey. Critics consider Joseph's consumption of alcoholic beverages hypocritical. Was it?

There is no doubt that Joseph drank alcohol before the Word of Wisdom was revealed. Martin Harris testified that Joseph "drank too much liquor" sometimes before he translated the Book of Mormon, which is acknowledged in Joseph's published history.[33] Most of the other evidence that Joseph drank before the Word of Wisdom comes from critics, including a statement by Barton Stafford that "Joseph Smith, Sen. was a noted drunkard and most of the family followed his example, and Joseph, Jr. especially, who was very much addicted to intemperance."[34] That seems exaggerated—*very much addicted.*

32. Joseph Smith address to the Mormons at Nauvoo on Last Sunday of April 1841, Reverend Julius A. Reed Collection, box 2 folder 15, Iowa State Historical Society, Iowa City, Iowa.

33. Joseph Smith Jr. , *History of the Church of Jesus Christ of Latter-day Saints*, ed. B. H. Roberts, 2nd ed., rev., 7 vols, (Salt Lake City: Deseret Book, 1971), 2:26 (hereafter cited as *History of the Church*).

34. Quoted in Rodger I. Anderson, *Joseph Smith's New York Reputation Reexamined* (Salt Lake City: Signature, 1989), 140.

Scholars have noted that Stafford was grinding an ax against Joseph, and that his statement seems inconsistent with the facts that Joseph's mother and siblings were upstanding Presbyterians, that Joseph translated the Book of Mormon, and that he attracted the principled Emma Hale and followers like the Whitmers, Knights, and other intelligent, moral people. A less hostile witness seems more credible. Orlando Saunders said that "everybody drank in those days," including the Smith family. "But," he added, "they never got drunk."[35] Joseph's father acknowledged in 1834 that he had been drunk in the past, but Saunders suggests, as one scholar noted, that "Joseph Sr.'s drinking was not excessive for that time and place."[36] Joseph Jr. acknowledged his drinking also. It was not unusual, nor yet forbidden by revelation. Maligning Joseph for drinking before the Word of Wisdom is silly and mean.

Emma Hale Smith (1804-1879) was the wife of LDS Church president Joseph Smith

What about Joseph's drinking after the Word of Wisdom was revealed in 1833? Joseph's journals are sprinkled with evidence of instances when he drank. There is a pattern. After marrying a couple in January 1836, Joseph joined the wedding party as they "partook of refreshments, and our hearts were made glad with the fruit of the vine." Speaking of the New Testament account of Christ furnishing a wedding party with wine, Joseph added playfully, "this is according to pattern set

35. Quoted in Anderson, *Joseph Smith's New York Reputation Reexamined*, 171.
36. Bushman, *Joseph Smith: Rough Stone Rolling*, 42.

by our Savior himself and we feel disposed to patronize all the institutions of heaven."[37] To Joseph, these were sacramental occasions. He drank wine at weddings in keeping with the Word of Wisdom's counsel to drink it "only in assembling yourselves together to offer up your sacraments before him. And, behold, this should be wine, yea, pure wine of the grape of the vine, of your own make" (D&C 89:5–6). The wine Joseph drank on these occasions had alcohol in it. Pure wine the Saints made themselves was wine, just as the wine Jesus made and used was wine. Originally, the Word of Wisdom approved, not condemned, such specific, moderate drinking of sacramental wine.

A week after the marriage mentioned above, Joseph officiated in another "matrimonial occasion," as his journal described it. After the ceremony, groomsmen supplied sacramental wine. Joseph said he "cheerfully" blessed it, and the wine "was then passed around in order, then the cake in the same order. Suffice it to say our hearts were made glad, while partaking of the bounty of the earth which was presented until we had taken our fill. Joy filled every bosom," Joseph wrote. "I doubt whether the pages of history can boast of a more splendid and innocent wedding and feast than this. For it was conducted after the order of heaven."[38]

Joseph also drank wine in sacramental settings in the Kirtland temple, but not all of the occasions on which he drank were sacramental. Joseph apparently had some whiskey while confined in jail at Liberty, Missouri, in the winter of 1838–1839.[39] His journal entry for May 3, 1843 notes that

---

37. Joseph Smith, Journal, January 14, 1836, Church History Library, Family and Church History Department, The Church of Jesus Christ of Latter-day Saints, Salt Lake City (hereafter cited as Church History Library).

38. Joseph Smith, Journal, January 18, 1836, Church History Library.

39. Peterson, "An Historical Analysis of the Word of Wisdom," 25.

Jenetta Richards, a recent immigrant from England and wife of apostle Willard Richards, visited his office with a bottle of wine her mother made in England. Joseph's journal says he "drank a glass of wine with her."[40] A month before his death, according to his journal, Joseph visited Frederick Moesser's grocery store and "drank a glass of beer."[41] On the last day of his life, confined in jail at Carthage, Illinois, solemn and conscious that he was about to meet his Maker, Joseph and his associates drank wine. John Taylor, an apostle who was with Joseph, frankly acknowledged and published in Joseph's official history that this was not a sacramental occasion. "Our spirits were generally dull and heavy," Taylor said, "and it was sent for to revive us." He said all four men in the jail "drank of the wine, and gave some to one or two of the prison guards."[42]

Critics have concluded based on this evidence that Joseph Smith and many of his followers did not live the Word of Wisdom. That conclusion is anachronistic, or out of historical order. It assumes that obedience for Joseph meant the same thing that it does today. That is demonstrably not the case. It is clear, however, that Joseph Smith knew the revelation well and observed it consciously if not always meticulously. He called intemperance a "monster," and "the bane of humanity." He "never interpreted the revelation as demanding total abstinence, but stressed moderation and self-control."[43] Joseph urged intemperate Saints to be temperate and teetotaling ones to be tolerant. Though Joseph rarely used tobacco, some unconfirmed evidence suggests that he may have once preached a discourse on the Word of Wisdom and then, to make a point, smoked a cigar.[44]

40. Joseph Smith, Journal, May 3, 1836, Church History Library.
41. Joseph Smith, Journal, June 1, 1844, Church History Library.
42. Joseph Smith, Junior, et al., *History of the Church of Jesus Christ of Latter-day Saints*, 7 volumes (Salt Lake City: Deseret, 1980), 7:101.
43. Peterson, "An Historical Analysis of the Word of Wisdom," 38.
44. Abraham Cannon, Journal, October 1, 1895, Church History Library.

Joseph would find it odd, though not unexpected, that critics seek out of his journal the handful of instances where he had a beer or drank a glass of homemade wine or enjoyed sacramental wine, or that he was tempted by whiskey, or that he drank some while he was unjustly imprisoned in a depressing dungeon. He would be puzzled that some people have focused inordinate attention on him and overlooked the Word of Wisdom itself. "I never told you I was perfect," Joseph said, "but there is no error in the revelations which I have taught."[45] It is not hard to find faults Joseph did not try to hide, but where are the flaws in the prophetic Word of Wisdom?

---

45. Joseph Smith, Sermon, May 12, 1844, as recorded in Thomas Bullock Diary, Church History Library.

How Did the Word of Wisdom Become a Commandment?

Latter-day Saints today are counseled not to drink anything alcoholic, and to abstain from tobacco, coffee and tea, harmful drugs, and to eat moderately according to the principles of the Word of Wisdom. Fellowship in the church is not dependent on keeping this counsel, but no one is knowingly baptized into the Church or admitted to Latter-day Saint temples for the highest forms of worship if they choose not to meet these basic requirements. Clearly there is a history of transition between the way Saints originally acted on the revelation and the way it is applied today. This chapter explores that transition.

A year after the Word of Wisdom was given, a question arose that led the Church to make a policy regarding it. Missionaries in Pennsylvania had refused to take the sacrament when they believed that the elder administering it did not obey the Word of Wisdom. When reports reached Kirtland, Ohio, the high council met to decide "whether disobedience to the Word of Wisdom was a transgression sufficient to deprive an official member from holding an office in the Church, after having it sufficiently taught him." Joseph Smith presided. Six counselors gave their views on the subject, and Joseph decided "that no official member in this Church is worthy to hold an office after having the Words of Wisdom properly taught to him, and he, the offi-

51

cial member, neglecting to comply with, or obey them." The council sustained this decision.[46]

What did it mean? It meant that one could not be an officer of the Church, that is, hold an official calling, if one chose not to obey the Word of Wisdom. And obeying in the 1830s meant abstaining generally if not absolutely from alcohol, coffee and tea, and tobacco. The policy did not mean that those who chose to disobey could not belong to the Church, just that they could not represent the Church or officiate in its ordinances if they had been property taught the Word of Wisdom and chose to disobey it. The Saints were free agents. Once they had knowledge to act upon, they were accountable for the choice they made. A choice to disobey resulted in losing the privilege to represent the Savior.

This basic policy has remained in effect until the present, though the years have seen several attempts to enforce the Word of Wisdom more strictly along with periods when it was hardly emphasized at all. Ever since the revelation was given to Joseph Smith in 1833, there have been a wide variety of responses to it in the Church. From the beginning there were, among the Church leaders and members, strict advocates like Sidney Rigdon and moderates like Joseph and Emma Smith, Brigham Young, and most of the Saints. There was also the occasional libertine who looked for any occasion to indulge excessively. Generally, this remains the pattern today.

Strict advocates grew out of the temperance movement. A notable example of this approach is an 1837 effort by the Seventies Quorum in Kirtland to enforce the Word of Wisdom among quorum members. Daniel Miles wrote, "If, as the Lord has said, strong drinks are not to be taken internally, can those who use them thus be held guiltless? We ask, if hot drinks are not to be used, if those who make use of them do not transgress

46. Kirtland Minute Book, February 20, 1834, Church History Library.

his commands, or at least set at nought his counsel? Most assuredly they do." Miles went on to remind his quorum members of Church policy. "Have not the authorities of the church in council assembled in this place, decided deliberately and positively that if any official member of this church shall violate or in any wise disregard the words of wisdom which the Lord has given for the benefit of his Saints, he shall lose his office? What official member does not know this? Brethren, either we believe this to be a revelation from God, or we do not. If we do not, we are acting the part of liars and hypocrites in the sight of God to say we are in the faith of the revelations and commandments of God which we have received. If we do, why disobey them and disregard them, and so live in open, avowed and acknowledged transgression, to our own soul's injury and the grief of our brethren?" Miles knew that some of his brethren blamed their disobedience on enslaving habits. "But," he argued, "we ask if the Almighty did not know your habits and the propensities of your nature? Certainly he did. Has he made any exceptions in your case, or are you wiser than he? Judge ye." To those who might have felt Miles was making too much of a minor issue, he asserted, "these, to many, may appear like small items; but to us, any transgression of the commands of God, or a disregard of what he has said, is evincive of a determination to gratify our own corrupt vitiated taste, the word of the Lord to the contrary notwithstanding."[47]

The seventies voted to withhold fellowship from any quorum members who drank distilled liquor, as well as those who wrestled, played ball, or similarly amused themselves. Joseph Smith would have admired the seventies loyalty to the revelation and their commitment to live by every word of God, but his own playful, freedom-loving personality would have chafed under the unrevealed restrictions the seventies imposed.

---

47. *Messenger and Advocate,* May 1837, 510–11.

Saints in the 1830s were often charged with violating the Word of Wisdom, but they were not denied fellowship except in rare cases of extreme or repeated intoxication.[48] With the founding of Nauvoo in 1839, Joseph and the Saints renewed commitment to the Word of Wisdom. The city council regulated liquor sales. In support of these laws, Joseph "spoke at great length on the use of liquors and showed that they were un-

necessary, and operate as a poison on the stomach, and that roots and herbs can be found to effect all necessary purposes."[49] Some Saints were denied fellowship by the Church and fined by the city when their efforts to sell liquor exceeded legal limits. But the demand for alcohol was great in Nauvoo, a Mississippi River town with many non-Mormon visitors and many Mormon residents still struggling to escape their longing for whiskey, whiskey, whiskey. Saints in Nauvoo generally, and Joseph specifically, relaxed efforts to regulate alcohol sales. Joseph even apparently considered selling liquor himself until Emma forbade it.[50] Apostle Heber Kimball advised Saints not to "nip and tuck at the Word of Wisdom, but stress the integrity of one's heart."[51] Meanwhile, the Saints accepting mission calls and other offices committed to "quit the use of tobacco and keep the Word of Wisdom," or stop the

Brigham Young was the successor of Joseph Smith, Jr. as prophet of the Church of Jesus Christ of Latter-day Saints.

Digital image © 2003 Utah State Historical Society. All Rights Reserved.

---

48. Peterson, "An Historical Analysis of the Word of Wisdom," 28–30.
49. *Times and Seasons* 2, February 15, 1841, 321.
50. Peterson, "An Historical Analysis of the Word of Wisdom," 32–34.
51. *Times and Seasons* 4, June 11, 1843, 316.

"use of tobacco and all spirituous liquors," at least "as much as possible."[52] If the Saints did not perfectly remember to keep the Word of Wisdom, they were more temperate than their neighbors.[53]

Brigham Young led the Church through a difficult pioneering period after Joseph's death. As a result of other pressing problems, Brigham did not expect strict adherence to the Word of Wisdom. "Could a man take a company of Saints to a desert and hold them to the task of building a community?" one analyst asked. "Then it didn't matter much to Brother Brigham if he was a user of whiskey and tobacco. Those Word of Wisdom virtues were precious to him but secondary."[54] Coffee was one of the most important supplies Saints took with them on the trek west. They consumed it like water under their heavy physical demands and lack of balanced nutrition and sufficient calories. Tea, tobacco, and alcohol were also in the wagons, handcarts, and finally the bodies of Latter-day Saint emigrants to the American west.

The Saints had not forgotten about the Word of Wisdom. Brigham Young and other leaders were regularly concerned about it. They established laws in Salt Lake to regulate the manufacture and sale of alcohol, and determined to renew Saints' efforts to obey. Outgoing missionaries were usually the most diligent, "preferring to observe the Word of Wisdom."[55] Non-Mormon visitors to Utah noted that the Saints were generally more temperate than their contemporaries. One noted that

52. Quoted in Peterson, "An Historical Analysis of the Word of Wisdom," 35.

53. Peterson, "An Historical Analysis of the Word of Wisdom," 36.

54. Nels Anderson, *Deseret Saints: The Mormon Frontier in Utah* (Chicago: University of Chicago Press, 1942), 439.

55. Richard Ballantyne, Journal, February 1853, volume 1, page 34, L. Tom Perry Special Collections, Harold B. Lee Library, Brigham Young University, Provo, Utah (hereafter cited as Perry Special Collections).

devout Saints abstained from alcohol and tobacco, "but occasionally they make no scruples of the moderate use of drink. Many of them take beer, to make which they cultivate hops in their valleys; others drink wine when they can get it, and some even indulge in whiskey, which they distill from the potato."[56] Generally, the middle decades of the nineteenth century were consumed with more pressing problems than getting the Saints to strictly obey the Word of Wisdom.

In the 1850s, Brigham Young and Church leaders began teaching younger Saints to observe the Word of Wisdom. Accepting the fact that many in his generation were addicted to

some or all of the prohibited substances, President Young thought that the next generation had been given sufficient knowledge to make them more accountable to observe the Word of Wisdom better. "If the old fogies take a little tobacco, a little whisky, or a little tea and coffee," he said, "we wish you boys to let it alone, and let those have it who have long been accustomed to its use." Brigham urged the boys who had begun chewing tobacco to stop it. "You young, smart gentlemen, let it alone," he urged.[57]

Emma Hale Smith (1804-1879) was the wife of LDS Church president Joseph Smith

During general conference in September 1851, President Young called upon the Saints to signify their willingness to observe the Word of Wisdom by raising their right hands. The Saints

56. Jules Remy and Julius Brenchley, *A Journey to Great Salt Lake City* (London: Jeffs, 1861), 1:271–72.
57. Brigham Young, in *Journal of Discourses*, 2:271, April 8, 1855. Peterson, "An Historical Analysis of the Word of Wisdom," 48–49.

overwhelmingly consented, and the First Presidency sent a letter to Saints abroad urging them to make the same commitment.[58] It took President Young himself another decade to finally conquer all of his habits, and he was lenient with the Saints who struggled similarly. In what must have been a hilarious sermon in April 1861, President Young distinguished between *Saints* who did not use tobacco, and *Mormons* who "use a vast quantity of it." He lamented that they were sending so much money out of the local economy by purchasing tobacco from abroad. If they were going to use it, he reasoned, then grow it locally. "We annually expend only $60,000 to break the 'Word of Wisdom,'" he said, "and we can save the money and still break it, if we will break it." President Young continued to make his points powerfully but gently. "A doctor told an old lady in New York, when she insisted upon his telling her whether snuff could injure her brain, 'It will not hurt the brain; there is no fear of snuff's hurting the brain of anyone, for no person that has brains will take snuff." He challenged the young men, saying if they were "manly enough to govern their appetites a little, they would not contract these bad habits." If the Saints were going to use tobacco, he urged them to be neat and judicious about it. "When you want another chew, down with it as you would a pill," he said. "It may make you vomit a little, but that is soon over. . . . That is the neatest way you can use tobacco."[59]

In this same 1861 sermon, President Young noted that "some of the brethren are very strenuous upon the 'Word of Wisdom' and would like to have me preach upon it, and urge it upon the brethren, and make it a test of fellowship. I do not think that I shall do so. I have never done so." Brigham never did make the Word of Wisdom a requirement for membership in the Church, but by July 1860 he had kicked his own tobac-

58. Peterson, "An Historical Analysis of the Word of Wisdom," 51–52.
59. Brigham Young, in *Journal of Discourses*, 9:35–36, April 7, 1861.

John Taylor (1808-1887) was a Methodist preacher who joined the LDS Church in England, was a pioneer, was imprisoned with Joseph and Hyrum Smith when they were killed, and served as the third President of the LDS Church from 1877-1887.

co habit and abstained from coffee, tea, and alcohol except for use as medicine. Moreover, he was increasingly concerned that the Saints were sending much needed money out of Utah to buy these "forbidden products."[60] He and other Church leaders began urging obedience to the Word of Wisdom for economic as well as religious reasons.[61] To Saints who complained they would die without tea, Brigham urged, "die in the faith, instead of living and breaking the requests of heaven." Of those who felt they would die without liquor or tobacco, Brigham said, "they will die with it, and they will die transgressing the revelations and commands of heaven, and the

wishes of our heavenly Father."[62] The Saints began to do better. Observers from both outside and inside the Church noted that obedience to the Word of Wisdom increased in the 1860s and 70s as a new generation was taught the Word of Wisdom from their youth.

Brigham Young himself exemplified the greater degree of diligence. "I have used tobacco a great portion of my life, and I have quit it," he told a group of Saints in 1861. At October general conference in 1862, he said it had been "two years and a half" since he had tasted tobacco. "I do not drink tea, coffee, nor intoxicating drinks," he added. In the late 1860s, President

60. Peterson, "An Historical Analysis of the Word of Wisdom," 58.
61. Leonard J. Arrington, "An Economic Interpretation of the Word of Wisdom," *BYU Studies* 1 (Winter 1959): 37–49.
62. Brigham Young, in *Journal of Discourses*, 14:20, May 6, 1870.

Young increasingly called on the Saints to abstain from harmful substances. His own conquest of addictions, the completion of the transcontinental railroad with its threats of draining Utah of needed resources, and increasing concern that the rising generation of Saints not be burdened with the addictions of their parents, moved President Young to lead what was probably "the Church's most earnest and sustained drive for Word of Wisdom reform to date."[63] As adherence improved among the Saints, President Young's wife Emily Partridge could still see significant room for improvement. She asked a series of penetrating questions: "Do we as a people realize the importance of those precious words? Do we accept them as the word of God unto us? Are they observed by this people as they should be? Could we find fifty Latter-day Saints in the Territory who abstain from tea, coffee, whiskey and tobacco or considers that it is worth while to even give it a thought? It is not high time to wake up and open our eyes and look about us? If the Lord had no purpose in giving the Word of Wisdom, why did he take the trouble to give it? And if it is not necessary for us to observe it, what is the use of having it."[64]

Wilford Woodruff served as the fourth president of the LDS Church from 1889-1898.

President John Taylor took up these questions in the early 1880s. More than ever before in Church history, he urged the Saints to obey the Word of

63. Paul H. Peterson and Ronald W. Walker, "Brigham Young's Word of Wisdom Legacy," *BYU Studies* 42:3–4 (2003): 47–48.

64. Emily Dow Partridge Young, Diary, L. Tom Perry Special Collections, Harold B. Lee Library, Brigham Young University.

Wisdom. Several states were adopting laws prohibiting the sale and manufacture of alcohol, which may have influenced President Taylor in the same ways the temperance movement influenced Joseph Smith to ask the Lord's will. President Taylor apparently received a revelation in the early 1880s that led him to reemphasize the Word of Wisdom. He asked for and received the support of his brethren in the First Presidency and Quorum of the Twelve Apostles. "We have come to the conclusion that we will more fully observe the word of wisdom," apostle Wilford Woodruff wrote, "as we have all been more or less negligent upon that point."[65] Church leaders emphasized obedience from the top down. As Paul Peterson wrote, "the time had come for Church members to observe the Word of Wisdom."[66] Reports rolled in from stake presidents, bishops, the Relief Society sisters and Primary leaders, all confirming "the marked disposition on the part of the Saints of late to keep the Word of Wisdom."[67]

Joseph F. Smith (1838-1918) was the son of early LDS Church leader, Hyrum Smith, president of the LDS Church from 1901-1918, and the father of future LDS Church president Joseph Fielding Smith.

Wilford Woodruff continued to emphasize the Word of Wisdom during his tenure as Church president. "The Word of Wisdom applies to Wilford Woodruff, the President of the

---

65. Minutes of the Salt Lake School of the Prophets, September 28, 1883, Church History Library.

66. Peterson, "An Historical Analysis of the Word of Wisdom," 73.

67. Peterson, "An Historical Analysis of the Word of Wisdom," 73–76.

Church," he declared in 1894, "and it applies to all the leaders of Israel as well as to the members of the Church; and if there are any of these leading men who cannot refrain from using tobacco or liquor in violation of the Word of Wisdom, let them resign and others take their places. As leaders of Israel, we have no business to indulge in these things. There may be things contrary to the Word of Wisdom that we cannot indulge in, and that we think we cannot live without; if we cannot, let us die."[68] In a May 1898 meeting, the First Presidency and some of the apostles discussed the Word of Wisdom at length. Lorenzo Snow had raised the question of whether bishops should issue temple recommends to Saints who did not obey the Word of Wisdom. After a full discussion, "President Woodruff said he regarded the Word of Wisdom in its entirety as given of the Lord for the Latter-day Saints to observe, but he did not think that Bishops should withhold recommends from persons who did not adhere strictly to it."[69]

Heber J. Grant was a businessman and a prominent Utahn. He was the first Utah born president of the LDS church, serving from 1918-1945.

Joseph F. Smith went a step further than Presidents Wilford Woodruff or Lorenzo Snow. He closed a Church-owned saloon, and led the First Presidency and apostles in June 1902 to a Church policy not to fellowship Saints who operated or frequented saloons. By

68. Quoted in Peterson, "An Historical Analysis of the Word of Wisdom," 77.
69. Diary of Heber J. Grant, quoted in Thomas G. Alexander, "The Word of Wisdom: From Principle to Requirement," *Dialogue* 14, no. 3 (1981), 78.

1905, President Smith urged stake presidents and bishops to be lenient toward elderly Saints who used coffee, tea, or tobacco, but to refuse temple recommends to Saints who flagrantly violated the Word of Wisdom. General authorities urged compliance in interviews with leaders and taught the Saints in stake conferences that the Church needed men in presiding positions who chose to obey. [70]

The movement to prohibit the manufacture and sale of alcohol gained momentum in the United States after 1906. Evangelical Protestants spearheaded the movement, but apostle Heber J. Grant actively supported and worked for its success in Utah. President Joseph F. Smith endorsed the movement in January 1908, but not all Church leaders or members agreed. Prohibition raised complex legal, political, economic, and moral issues. A revelation that left agency in individual Saints was one thing, but some Saints were uncertain if governments could appropriately prohibit alcohol. There were both petty and legitimate political arguments and concerns, even among Latter-day Saints. Still, prohibition continued to gain political momentum and became a law in Utah in 1917. A bill prohibiting tobacco use passed the Utah state legislature in 1921, but it was widely disobeyed. Still, throughout the 1920s and 1930s, Church leaders urged abstinence from tobacco on moral and scientific grounds.

In the Church, President Joseph F. Smith continued to urge obedience. He tolerated the habits of elderly Saints while declaring in 1915 that young and middle-aged men "who have experience in the Church should not be ordained to the Priesthood nor recommended to the privileges of the House of the Lord unless they will abstain from the use of tobacco and intoxicating drinks."[71] Joseph F. Smith was the last Church presi-

---

70. Alexander, "The Word of Wisdom: From Principle to Requirement," 79.
71. Joseph F. Smith to C. Elmo Cluff, December 28, 1915, Joseph F. Smith Letterbooks, Church History Library.

dent who personally knew Joseph Smith, his uncle. His death in 1918 signaled that the generation of Saints alive before the Word of Wisdom was given had nearly all passed away. New president Heber J. Grant thereafter made obedience to basic prohibitions of alcohol, tobacco, tea and coffee requirements for temple worship. By 1933, the handbook of instructions for stake presidents and bishops explicitly said that Saints desiring to attend the temple "should keep the Word of Wisdom," whereas an earlier version had simply said they should obey "Gospel principles." Church leaders were also advised that Saints guilty of drunkenness or illegally making or selling alcohol could be subject to Church discipline.[72]

No president of the Church taught the Word of Wisdom more than Heber J. Grant. He presided over the Church as prohibition on the manufacture and sale of alcohol was repealed in the United States, much to his disappointment. Tobacco consumption skyrocketed during the 1930s and 1940s. The Word of Wisdom was emphasized more during this period of the Church's history than any before or since. Though President Grant often felt frustrated at the Saints for their general weakness relative to the Word of Wisdom, obedience among the Saints increased, counter to national trends. President Grant fought hard and, in the end, exerted a remarkable influence against the powerful forces of alcohol and tobacco.

So when exactly did the Word of Wisdom become a commandment? The answer depends on what one means by *commandment*. If one means, when did the Lord express his will that Saints obey the Word of Wisdom, then the answer is, the day he gave it, February 27, 1833. If one means, when did the Church begin forcing Saints to obey, the answer is never. The Church has never *required* anyone to obey the Word of Wisdom, ever. The Lord revealed wisdom to the Saints and expect-

72. Alexander, "The Word of Wisdom: From Principle to Requirement," 84.

ed them to obey, from the beginning, as best they could. Some claim it became binding in 1851, when Brigham Young asked for and received the Saints' sustaining vote to obey. President Young himself struggled for another decade to give up tobacco. Some claim it became binding in the 1880s, when President John Taylor emphasized obedience again.

If no single date can be established when the Lord made obedience to the Word of Wisdom binding upon Latter-day Saints, his merciful forewarning and longsuffering with weakness is clear. The Lord's prophets have consistently applied the principle of agency, always urging obedience yet making allowances for those who were acted upon by powerful substances before they had enough knowledge to act intelligently for themselves. Joseph F. Smith, who had himself struggled with chewing tobacco as a young man, believed that if the Word of Wisdom was strictly enforced in the nineteenth century "it would have brought every man addicted to the use of these noxious things under condemnation; so the Lord was merciful and gave them a chance to overcome, before he brought them under the law."[73]

Some claim that the Word of Wisdom finally became binding when President Heber J. Grant made obedience a requirement for obtaining a temple recommend. He approached obedience, however, as a principle of individual agency. President Grant taught that obedience to the Word of Wisdom resulted from love for God rather than a constraining command. "If you love God with all your heart, might, mind and strength, does he need to command?" President Grant asked.[74] The Word of Wisdom is still not binding. No one is bound to obey it anymore than they are bound to not steal, lie, commit adultery, to observe the Sabbath, or to love God and their neighbor. And in one way or another, many still fall short.

73. Joseph F. Smith, *Conference Report*, October 1913, 14.
74. Quoted in Peterson, "An Historical Analysis of the Word of Wisdom," 98.

How Does the Church Interpret and Apply the Word of Wisdom Today?

The Church interprets the Word of Wisdom today as it is found in Doctrine and Covenants section 89, with the understanding that hot drinks refer to tea and coffee, and that Saints should now completely abstain from all alcoholic beverages. The Church applies the Word of Wisdom today by asking all members to live it.[75] Converts seeking baptism into the Church and Latter-day Saints seeking a recommend to worship in the temple are asked whether they obey the Word of Wisdom.[76] A minimal standard of abstaining from alcohol, coffee, tea, and tobacco is considered sufficient compliance.

While the Church's official position, noted above, is quite simple, questionable new products or changing historical circumstances lead Saints to ask new questions and Church leaders to clarify. In 1917, an article by Frederick Pack in the Church's *Improvement Era* posed the question, "Should LDS Drink Coca-Cola?" He argued no, given that it contained caffeine, as did tea and coffee. Coca-Cola representa-

The Coca-cola sign on the Temple Pharmacy.

75. Gordon B. Hinckley, "Latter-day Counsel: Selections from Addresses of President Gordon B. Hinckley," *Ensign*, February 2002, 49.
76. Packer, "The Word of Wisdom: The Principle and the Promises," 17.

tives contacted President Heber J. Grant with concerns that the Church was against their product. President Grant refused to take an official position one way or the other, leaving the issue to principle. Church leaders since have followed his lead. "We teach the principle together with the promised blessings," Elder Boyd K. Packer declared. What is the principle? The list of prohibitions includes alcohol, tobacco, coffee, tea, and harmful drugs. Together with these, all other habit-forming substances should be avoided. Obedience to this principle preserves individual agency. The obedient qualify for the promised blessings of health, wisdom, and deliverance.[77]

Ever since the Word of Wisdom was given, some Saints have given it a very close reading in order to justify habits. They are sometimes the best experts on the technical wording of the revelation—including the placement of punctuation. This type of person reads the revelation as a legal code, discerning precisely what they can get away with, not necessarily what is best for their temporal salvation. Brigham Young noted that "many try to excuse themselves because tea and coffee are not mentioned, arguing that it refers to hot drinks only. What did we drink when that Word of Wisdom was given? Tea and coffee."[78] A missionary addicted to caffeine taught potential Saints that coffee and tea were prohibited because they contained tannic acid, not caffeine. One frustrated, self-described "Diet Coke Lover" weighed in: "I drink diet coke all the time. It is an INSIGNIFICANT part of my life. I hold a temple recommend, because again, caffeine is an insignificant part of my life. Do we really need to feel guilty over something like this? I know many Mormons who focus specifically on this point as if by not drinking caffeine they have a special 'Me First' marker on their ticket to Heaven. Most of the people I've

---

77. Peterson, "An Historical Analysis of the Word of Wisdom," 101. Alexander, "The Word of Wisdom: From Principle to Requirement," 84.
78. Brigham Young, in *Journal of Discourses*, 12:117, August 17, 1867.

known who are so uptight about drinking caffeine and focus on this as a sin and are happy to point it out to anyone who will listen, have committed far worse sins in their life. They just don't have a problem with caffeine so they use that as a most important point in righteousness. Grow up and GET OVER IT!!!"[79] This person might have a valid point, but meanwhile sounds like someone for whom caffeine is indeed significant. Perhaps they have had too much. Whether this writer needs to feel guilty for this habit, it sounds like they do. Moreover, the statement is ironically judgmental of those who are judgmental. "There are many habit-forming, addictive things that one can drink or chew or inhale or inject which injure both body and spirit which are not mentioned in the revelation," wrote Elder Boyd K. Packer. "Everything harmful is not specifically listed; arsenic, for instance—certainly bad, but not habit-forming! He who must be commanded in all things, the Lord said, 'is a slothful and not a wise servant (D&C 58:26).'"[80] President Gordon B. Hinckley and others have noted the terrible toll of drug abuse, and have urged Saints to abstain completely from illicit drugs. He noted that some excused drug abuse by arguing that the Word of Wisdom does not prohibit it. "What a miserable excuse," President Hinckley declared. "There is likewise no mention of the hazards of diving into an empty swimming pool or of jumping from an overpass onto the freeway. But who doubts the deadly consequences of such? Common sense would dictate against such behavior."[81]

Church members interpret and apply the Word of Wisdom individually. This is true not only of some seeking to justify bad habits, but of some seeking support for personal agendas. Some individual Saints or private groups have urged their views

---

79. www.meridianmagazine.com/letters/010427softdrink.html.
80. Packer, "The Word of Wisdom: The Principle and the Promises," 17.
81. Gordon B. Hinckley, "The Scourge of Illicit Drugs," *Ensign*, November 1989, 48; Nelson, "Addiction or Freedom," 6.

on others, citing the Word of Wisdom as their authority. A billboard near Salt Lake City featured a Moses-like figure forbidding the consumption of meat, citing D&C 89:12–15 (but conveniently not D&C 49:19). Some have prohibited chocolate or refined sugar. One isolated group of Saints wanted to withdraw fellowship from another group who ate white bread. An influential speaker tried to persuade an audience of the virtues of a no-grain diet. The speaker misread D&C 89:14–15 (the passage that says grain should be the staff of life, and that God made wild animals for mankind to use in times of excessive hunger) and made it sound like grains were to be used only in times of excessive hunger. Joseph Smith urged intemperate Saints to be temperate and teetotaling ones to be tolerant. Modern prophets urge addicted Saints to gain control of their habits and all Saints to beware of "stretching the Word of Wisdom to conform with our own opinions."[82]

Some children, youth, and even adults lack a sense of the relative importance of the Word of Wisdom. A woman who was studying the gospel came to a sacrament meeting. She had not yet been taught the Word of Wisdom. She struggled with a tobacco habit and drank coffee. The hymn that day announced, "tea and coffee and tobacco we despise."[83] She never came back. To her the hymn said, "whoever drinks tea and coffee or takes tobacco we despise." Children of Latter-day Saints might mistakenly regard a smoker or coffee-drinker as evil indeed. Some teens who would never smoke or drink might violate the comparatively much more crucial law of chastity. These errors need to be corrected. But the Word of Wisdom is no light matter. Habitual use of seemingly innocuous substances

---

82. John A. Widtsoe, *Evidences and Reconciliations*, 3 vols. (Salt Lake City: Bookcraft, 1951), 3:155.

83. "In Our Lovely Deseret," in Hymns of The Church of Jesus Christ of Latter-day Saints (Salt Lake City, The Church of Jesus Christ of Latter-day Saints, 1985), no. 307.

can lead to dependence and thence to far greater, potentially deadly, behaviors. The Word of Wisdom is not the most important aspect of the gospel, but those whose love for God inspires them to live the gospel strive to adhere to the Word of Wisdom in letter and in spirit.

The Lord adapted the Word of Wisdom to the Saints (D&C 89:3). Joseph Smith, Brigham Young, and their successors have interpreted and applied the Word of Wisdom pragmatically to the circumstances of the Saints over whom they presided. As historical circumstances foreseen by the Lord have unfolded, the Lord's prophets have adapted the Word of Wisdom to the needs and capacities of the Saints. It is living wisdom rather than a dead law.

Epilogue:
Not by Constraint

There is a widespread and mistaken notion that God's will generally and the Word of Wisdom specifically are constraining. T-shirts are occasionally seen saying: "I can't. I'm Mormon." This is not theologically accurate. Mormons can do whatever they want. They do. The restored gospel generally and the Word of Wisdom specifically are calculated to increase our agency, the power to knowingly act for ourselves. Choosing to obey the Word of Wisdom is not like a game show, where the choice is an uninformed gamble. The revelation is specific knowledge. An all-knowing God tells us that distilled beverages are not good to ingest, nor is wine, nor tobacco, coffee, or tea. He counsels us to eat healthful foods prudently, in the right proportions and seasons, and with gratitude. He forewarns us that conspiring men will try to deceive us. Knowing all this, we can choose to be spared from several different destroyers. Those who obey the revelation generally live longer, healthier lives than those who do not.[84] Still, Latter-day Saints decide for themselves what they will do with the Word of Wisdom. Perhaps the T-shirt should say, "I won't. I'm Mormon."

One might ask, since God foresaw evils and designs in the hearts of conspiring men in the last days, why didn't he stop them. One answer is agency. He gives us all freedom to do evil as well as good, or else there is no freedom at all. The Lord

---

84. Hinckley, "Latter-day Counsel," 49.

uses his omniscience to preserve agency by giving wisdom and knowledge for people to do with as they will. He could send bugs to destroy tobacco crops, but tobacco is not evil. It has no agency. It has legitimate uses. It is the illegitimate use of it by free agents, and the potential of that action to weaken or destroy agency, that concerns the Lord. Could the Lord make it impossible to produce alcohol? Certainly, but alcohol is not itself bad. The Lord denounces taking alcohol into one's body, together with whatever evils and designs exist in the hearts of people. The Word of Wisdom concerns the actions of free agents. It teaches them how to be wise stewards, informed about their world, its wonderfully useful resources, and the potentially evil uses to which these can be put by conspirators with evil designs.

Yes, the Lord could have put an end to the conspiracies aimed at enslaving his children, but that might have had the ironic, unintended consequence of undermining individual agency. Instead he informs. This puts all of the elements of agency to work—liberty and power to act, knowledge of how to act, opposition to that knowledge, and thus choice. The Lord gave agency in the Word of Wisdom, not constraint. If the Lord had not revealed the Word of Wisdom when and how he did, the agency of many might have been taken by the conspirators. By giving the revelation, God preserved both their agency and ours. Of those who knew the Word of Wisdom, the conspiracies have only been able to enslave volunteers of their own free will and, alas, bad choices. One addicted young man told his ironic story. "He said that one day when he was feeling despondent and discouraged, he decided that he wanted to be free, that he did not want to be bound by any traditions or Church restrictions in any way. In a spirit of rebellion, he went out one day with some fellows who took drugs—and then he said: 'Here I am. Instead of being free, I'm a slave.'"[85]

"You have the 'Word of Wisdom,'" said Brigham Young. "Read it." He taught that "there is not a single Saint deprived of the privilege of asking the Father, in the name of Jesus Christ our Savior," whether the prophets have taught the truth in the Word of Wisdom, and gaining their own conviction by the power of the Holy Ghost. [86] Those who study it carefully and apply its principles find, as President Gordon B. Hinckley taught, that "it doesn't impose burdens on us. It gives us blessings."[87] It has never been given "by commandment or constraint, but by revelation" to help us be wise if we should so choose (D&C 89:2), "not to put shackles on us."[88] It was not constraining when it was given in 1833, and it is not constraining now. Those who choose to obey it are extraordinarily free and have considerable power over their own health, opportunities, and destinies. It is true that Latter-day Saints feel social pressure to obey the Word of Wisdom. They also feel social pressure not to. The pressures come from all sides. They make us free to choose between them. We not only can but must choose what we will do, individually, with the Word of Wisdom.

85. N. Eldon Tanner, "Trusting the Lord's Promise," *Ensign*, August 1981, 2.

86. Brigham Young, in *Journal of Discourses*, 8:361 and 12:117, March 10, 1860 and August 17, 1867.

87. Hinckley, "Latter-day Counsel," 49.

88. Hinckley, "Latter-day Counsel," 71.

Appendix A:
Hyrum Smith, "The Word of Wisdom,"
Times and Seasons 3, June 1, 1842.

THE WORD OF WISDOM

We had a very instructive, impressive, and salutary discourse delivered us in the City of Nauvoo, last Sabbath on the above subject, to a large and attentive congregation, by Pres't. Hyrum Smith.

He stated "that there were many of the commands of God that seemed to be overlooked by this generation, and he was fearful that many of the Latter Day Saints in this respect were following their old tradition, and former practices of spiritualizing the word of God, and through a vain philosophy departing from the pure principles of eternal truth which God had given by revelation for the salvation of the human family; but, that every word of God is of importance, whether it be the word contained in the Bible, in the Book of Mormon, or in the Book of Doctrine and Covenants, for 'man shall not live by bread alone, but by every word that proceedeth from the mouth of God.' The principles that are taught in the Bible are pure, and ought to be adhered too; and if people adhere to that teaching it will prove their salvation. The principles that are taught in the Book of Mormon are also pure, and holy and righteous, and will if followed lead men to God. And the principles that are taught in the Book of Doctrine and Covenants, are from God, they are principles of righteousness;-they are given for a blessing to the human family, and the salvation, temporal and spiritual, of his saints; and that man who wantonly departs from any of the revelations of Jehovah, and treats lightly the word of God, whether contained in the Book of Doctrine and Covenants, the Book of Mormon, or the Bible, is void of understanding: he is not wise concerning the doings of the Lord, the plan of salvation, the past dealings, present designs, or future purposes of the Almighty. The God of the armies of Israel is a wise God, he comprehended the end from the beginning, and adapted his plans, his designs and teaching, to the peculiar wants, the local situation, the exigencies of mankind; and the present and future good of the human family; and every thing that he has deigned to notice by way of instruction to the children of men, is given by infinite wisdom; by the intelligence of Jehovah; and if obeyed, when his designs shall be fully unraveled, it will be seen that there was wisdom in it beyond the comprehension of man in his present state.

When God first made man upon the earth, he was a different being entirely to what he now is; his body was strong; athletic, robust, and healthy; his days were prolonged upon the earth; he lived nearly one thousand years, his mind was vigorous and active, and his intellectual faculties clear and comprehensive, but he has become degenerated; his life has dwindled to a span; disease preys upon his system; his body is enervated and feeble; and his mental and intellectual faculties are impaired, and weakened; and man is not now that dignified, noble, majestic, honorable, and mighty being that he was when he first proceeded from the hands of his maker.

The Lord has in his wise designs revealed unto us his will; he has told us as he did his ancient prophets that the 'earth shall be redeemed-that the curse shall be removed from it-that the wolf and the lamb shall lie down together-that the lion shall eat straw like the ox;-and that they shall not hurt nor destroy-that the knowledge of the Lord shall cover the earth, as the waters covers the sea'-that man's days shall be as the 'days of a tree,' that he shall again live one thousand years on the earth-this is the 'time of the restoration of all things,' and this has got to be brought about by the wisdom and power of God, and the wisdom, obedience and faith of man combined.

Every thing has become degenerated from what it was in its primitive state; 'God made man pure, but he has found out many inventions:' his vices have become innumerable, and his diseases multiplied; his taste had become vitiated, and his judgment impaired; he has fallen-fallen-fallen, from that dignified state that he once occupied on the earth; and it needs a restorative that man has not in his possession-wisdom which is beyond the reach of human intellect;-and power which human philosophy, talent and ingenuity cannot control. God only is acquainted with the fountain of action, and the main springs of human events; he knows where disease is seated, and what is the cause of it;-he is also acquainted with the spring of health; the balm of Gilead-of life; he knows what course to pursue to restore mankind to their pristine excellency and primitive vigour, and health; and he has appointed the word of wisdom as one of the engines to bring about this thing, to remove the beastly appetites, the murderous disposition and the vitiated taste of man; to restore his body to health, and vigour, promote peace between him and the brute creation, and as one of the little wheels in God's designs, to help to regulate the great machinery, which shall eventually revolutionize the earth, and bring about the restoration of all things, and when they are restored he will plant 'the tree of life, whose leaves shall be for the healing of the nations.'

The Lord has told us what is good for us to eat, and to drink, and what is pernicious; but some of our wise philosophers, and some of our elders too, pay no regard to it; they think it too little, too foolish, for wise men to regard fools! where is their wisdom, philosophy and intelligence? from whence did they obtain their superior light? Their capacity, and their power of reasoning was given them by the great Jehovah: if they have any wisdom they obtained it from his: and have they grown so much wiser than God that they are going to instruct him in the path of duty, and to tell him what is wise, and what is foolish. They think it too small for him to condescend [condescend] to tell men what will be nutritious or what will be unhealthy. Who made the corn, the wheat, the rye, and all the vegetable substances? and who was it that organized man, and constituted him as he is found? who made his stomach, and his digestive organs, and prepared proper nutriment for his system, that the juices of his body might be supplied; and his form be invigorated by that kind of food which the laws of nature, and the laws of God has said would be good for man? And has God made his food, and provided it for the use of man; and shall he be ashamed to speak of the work of his hands: has he become so fantastical, so foolish, so weak and effeminate, that it has become impolitic for him to tell what is the best distribution to make of the work of his hands? Oh shame! let it not be heard among the saints; let that man who inculcates such principles hide his face. We are told by some that circumstances alter the revelations of God-tell me what circumstances would alter the ten commandments? they were given by revelation-given as a law to the children of Israel;-who has a right to alter that law? Some think that they are too small for us to notice, they are not too small for God to notice, and have we got so high, so bloated out, that we cannot condescend to notice things that God has ordained for our benefit? or have we got so weak that we are not fit to be called saints? for the word of wisdom is adapted to the capacity of all that 'are or can be called saints.' Listen not to the teaching of any man, or any elder who says the word of wisdom is of no moment; for such a man will eventually be overthrown.

These are principles that I have always acted upon; that I have always practiced; and they are what my family practices; they are what Brother Hyrum has always contended for, and what I now contend for; and I know that nothing but an unwavering, undeviating course can save a man in the kingdom of God.

The Lord has told us that 'Strong drinks are not good,' who is it that will say they are? when the Lord says they are not. That man who says 'I can drink wine or strong drink, and it will not hurt me,' is not wise. But some will say, 'I know it did me good, for I was fatigued, and feeble, on a certain occasion, and it revived me, and I was invigorated thereby, and that is sufficient proof for me:' It may be for you, but it would not be for a wise man, for every spirit of this kind will only produce a greater languor when its effects cease to operate upon the human body. But you know that you are benefited, yes, so does the man who has mortgaged his property, know that he is relieved from his present embarrassments; but his temporary relief only binds the chords of bondage more severely around him. The Lord has not ordained strong drink for the belly; 'but for the washing of your bodies.' And again 'tobacco is not for the body, neither for the belly; and it is not good for man; but as an herb for bruises, and all sick cattle, to be used with judgment and skill.' Tobacco is a nauseous, stinking abominable thing, and I am surprised that any human being should think of using it-for an elder especially to eat, or smoke it, is a disgrace to him;-he is not fit for the office, he ought first to learn to keep the word of wisdom, and then to teach others. God will not prosper the man who uses it. And again 'hot drinks are not for the body, or belly;' there are many who wonder what this can mean; whether it refers to tea, or coffee, or not. I say it does refer to tea, and coffee. Why is it that we are frequently so dull and languid? it is because we break the word of wisdom, disease preys upon our system, our understandings are darkened, and we do not comprehend the things of God; the devil takes advantage of us, and we fall into temptation. Not only are they injurious in their tendency, and baneful in their effects, but the importation of foreign products might be the means of thousands of our people being poisoned at a future time, through the advantage that an enemy might take of us, if we made use of these things that are thus spoken of as being evil; and be it remembered-that this instruction is given 'in consequence of evils that do and will exist in the hearts of conspiring men.'

'And again, verily I say unto you, all wholesome herbs God hath ordained for the constitution, nature and use of man. Every herb in the season thereof, and every fruit in the season thereof. All these to be used with prudence and thank giving [thanksgiving]. Yea, flesh also of beasts and of the fowls of the air, I the Lord hath ordained for the use of man with thanksgiving. Nevertheless, they are to be used sparingly; and it is pleasing unto me, that they should not be used only in times of winter or of cold, or famine. All grain is ordained for the use of man, and of beasts, to be the staff of life, not only for man, but for the beasts of the field, and the fowls of heaven, and all wild animals that run or creep on the earth; and these hath God made for the use of man only in times of famine, and excess of hunger.'

Let men attend to these instructions, let them use the things ordained of God; let them be sparing of the life of animals; 'it is pleasing saith the Lord that flesh be used only in times of winter, or of famine'-and why to be used in famine? because all domesticated animals would naturally die, and may as well be made use of by man, as not,

"All grain is good for the food of man, as also the fruit of the vine, that which yieldeth fruit, whether in the ground or above the ground Nevertheless wheat for man, and corn for the ox, and oats for the horse, and rye for the fowls, and barley for all useful animals, and for mild drinks; as also other grain. And all saints who remember to keep and do these sayings, walking in obedience to the commandments, shall receive health in their naval, and marrow in their bones and shall find wisdom, and great treasures of knowledge even hidden treasures; and shall run and not be weary, and shall walk and not faint: and I the Lord give unto them a promise, that the destroying angel shall pass by them, as the children of Israel, and not slay them. Amen.'

Let these things be adhered to; let the saints be wise; let us lay aside our folly and abide by the commandments of God; so shall we be blessed of the great Jehovah in time and in eternity: we shall be healthy, strong and vigorous: we shall be enabled to resist disease; and wisdom will crown our councils, and our bodies will become strong and powerful, our progeny will become mighty, and will rise up and call us blessed; the daughters of Jesus will be beautiful, and her sons the joy of the whole earth; we shall prepare ourselves for the purposes of Jehovah for the kingdom of God for the appearance of Jesus in his glory; "out of Zion the perfection of beauty," God will shine; Zion will be exalted, and become the praise of the whole earth."

Thus spake the man of God, fired with heavenly holy zeal, for the welfare of the saints of the most high, who were assembled around him, in breathless silence, listening to the gracious words that fell from his lips, which we feel ourselves utterly incapable of doing justice to, in this brief sketch; and can only say that with boldness and firmness he expatiated freely and fully upon those principles opposing vice and error in its various forms; we are persuaded that his instructions will be indelibly engraven on the memories of thousands who listened to his discourse. Firm and unwavering in his principles, he has ever been the advocate of sterling integrity, righteousness and truth, and when we saw him exerting all his energies to impress upon the minds of the audience the importance of the thing that he advocated, it reminded us of the sayings of one of the ancient servants of God. "I will declare thy righteousness in the great congregation.'

OMEGA.

Appendix B:

Excerpts from Remarks by President Brigham Young, in *Journal of Discourses*, 26 vols. (Liverpool: F. D. Richards, 1855–86), 9:31–40, April 7, 1861.

I wish to speak upon what pertains to our temporal affairs, which I would very well have liked to have been brought before the Bishops meeting without detaining a congregation like this on such matters. I wish to urge upon the people the necessity of providing for themselves, and not being dependent entirely upon others.

The Lord has given us ability to do a great many things. What a blessing this is! Do you ever think of it? A man has ability to take the raw materials and build a good, comfortable habitation for the accommodation of himself; his wives, and children. The wife can spread a table with wholesome food, and in a manner pleasant to the eye, while the food is gratifying to the palate. They have the ability to provide, if they choose, downy beds upon which to rest their weary bodies. Do you ever think of this? I presume the greater part of the inhabitants of the earth have lived and died without reflecting much upon whence they derived this ability, to whom they were indebted for the ingenuity they possess, or the capability that is organized within them to gather around them the comforts of life. Do you, brethren, think of it?

We have ability to cultivate the earth; we know how to raise stock, how to make clothing, and are not obliged to go naked like the Indians. We are not obliged to lie down in the open air with perhaps a few sage brush around us, as do many of the natives. We have ability to make ourselves comfortable as to the physical wants of this life. Where did we get that ability? Are your hearts lifted to the Donor of those blessings? Do you remember from whence your ability came? Who organized these tabernacles? Who put into them these thinking powers? Who has placed the spirit in the body, and organized them together, and made us capable of reflecting? Where did you get this ability? A well-read historian and geographical scholar can contemplate his antipodes, and in his mind see what they are doing. He can also behold the various exhibitions of human skill in different nations; both in their social and political capacity; for they are in the vision of his mind. Who gave the ability to reflect and to behold the earth and the inhabitants thereof? Is not this a blessing? How cheering, how comforting, how consoling, how exalting! I would be glad if we could realize the blessings we possess.

The Lord has placed in our possession the elements pertaining to this earth. As I told the people, when we first came into this Valley in 1847, there is plenty of silk in the elements here, as much so as in any other part of the earth. Here is also the fine linen. Were there any sheep here when we came first here? No. Were there any silk raisers then here? No. Were there any flax raisers here? No; neither was there a stalk of flax growing, except what was growing wild. The elements are here. Bring the seeds, the eggs of the silkworm, raise the trees for feeding the worms, and let us see if we cannot produce silk here. It is in the elements. We have the elements to produce as good wheat as grows. The elements here will produce the apple, the peach, the pear, the plum, the apricot, the cherry, the currant, and every kind of fruit in abundance, and every variety of plant and vegetable we desire. Have you the ability to bring any of these things forth from the native element? Yes; here are men who know how to raise fruit, and here are the women who know how to dry and cook it. Here are the men who know how to raise sheep, and how to take their fleeces and deliver them into the hands of their families to be manufactured. Here are women who know how to spin, weave, and make the finest of cloth. So with the flax, and so with every material calculated to make us comfortable. Where did we get this ability? We got it from our Father who is in heaven. Be thankful for these precious gifts. As brother Kimball justly said, "Remember, first of all, the Giver;" worship and adore the Giver. Some will lose a great deal by neglecting the Giver and by worshipping the gift. Such will find that they will meet with losses. . . . .

You know that we all profess to believe the "Word of Wisdom." There has been a great deal said about it, more in former than in latter years. We, as Latter-day Saints, care but little about tobacco; but, as "Mormons," we use a vast quantity of it. As Saints, we use but little; as "Mormons," we use a great deal. How much do you suppose goes annually from this Territory, and has for ten or twelve years past, in gold and silver, to supply the people with tobacco? I will say $60,000. Brother William H. Hooper, our Delegate in Congress, came here in 1849, and during about eight years he was selling goods his sales for tobacco alone amounted to over $28,000 a year. At the same time there were other stores that sold their share and drew their share of the money expended yearly, besides what has been brought in by the keg and by the half keg. The traders and passing emigration have sold tons of tobacco, besides what is sold here regularly. I say that $60,000 annually is the smallest figure I can estimate the sales at. Tobacco can be raised here as well as it can be raised in any other place. It wants attention and care. If we use it, let us raise it here. I recommend for some man to go to raising tobacco. One man who came here last fall, is going to do so; and if he is diligent, he will raise quite a quantity. I want to see some man go to and make a business of raising tobacco and stop sending money out the Territory for that article.

Some of the brethren are very strenuous upon the "Word of Wisdom," and would like to have me preach upon it, and urge it upon the brethren, and make it a test of fellowship. I do not think that I shall do so. I have never done so. We annually expend only $60,000 to break the "Word of Wisdom" and we can save the money and still break it, if we will break it. Some would ask brother Brigham whether he keeps the "Word of Wisdom." No: and I can say still further, as I told one of the teachers in Nauvoo, I come as near doing so as any man in this generation. It is not using tobacco that particularly breaks the "Word of Wisdom" nor is that the only bad practice it corrects; but it is profitable in every path of life. If our young persons were manly enough to govern their appetites a little, they would not contract these bad habits; but they must have some weaknesses; they must not be perfect and exactly right in everything. It is a loathsome practice to use tobacco in any way. A doctor told an old lady in New York, when she insisted upon his telling her whether snuff would injure her brain, "It will not hurt the brain: there is no fear of snuff's hurting the brain of anyone, for no person that has brains will take snuff." I will say that the most filthy way of using tobacco is to smoke it. What is the neat way? If you are going to direct any course for the people to use tobacco, let us know what it is. Cannot you who have used it for years point out a neat, modest, judicious way of using it? The "Word of Wisdom" says that tobacco is good for sick cattle; and when you want another chew, down with it as you would a pill. It may make you vomit a little, but that is soon over, and it is good for sick cattle. That is the neatest way you can use tobacco.

Appendix C:

"Observing the Word of Wisdom,"
Teachings of Presidents of the Church, Heber J. Grant
(Salt Lake City: The Church of Jesus Christ
of Latter-day Saints, 2002), 189–98.

The Lord gave us the Word of Wisdom for our temporal and spiritual salvation.

From the Life of Heber J. Grant

During President Heber J. Grant's service as an Apostle and as President of the Church, he and other General Authorities often were inspired to address the Saints concerning the Word of Wisdom, a revelation found in Doctrine and Covenants 89. In this revelation, the Lord prohibits the consumption of alcohol, tobacco, and hot drinks, which latter-day prophets have defined to be tea and coffee (see D&C 89:5–9). The Lord also says that wholesome herbs, grains, and fruits are "ordained for the use of man," along with meat, which is "to be used sparingly" (see D&C 89:10–17). In addition to exhorting the Saints to obey this specific counsel, President Grant and other Presidents of the Church have spoken out against the use of harmful or habit-forming substances such as illegal drugs. President Grant said, "The Lord does not want you to use any drug that creates an appetite for itself."[1]

Much of President Grant's motivation for preaching the Word of Wisdom came because he had a friend whose life was ruined by cigarettes and liquor. This young man gave up smoking so he could serve a mission, but he started to smoke immediately after his release from full-time missionary service.

Smoking led to liquor drinking, and liquor drinking led to a loss of virtue and to excommunication from the Church. He died at a young age, and Heber J. Grant went to visit his grave. "As I stood at his grave," President Grant recalled, "I looked up to heaven and made a pledge to my God that liquor and tobacco would have in me an enemy who would fight with all the ability that God would give me until the day of my death."[2]

Some members of the Church in President Grant's day complained about the numerous sermons they heard on the Word of Wisdom. President Grant commented: "There is seldom a conference when someone does not take it upon himself to tell us: 'Please do not speak on the Word of Wisdom. We hear it so much, we are sick and tired of it.' " President Grant responded to such complaints by saying: "No mortal man who is a Latter-day Saint and is keeping the Word of Wisdom is ever sick and tired of hearing it. When a man leaves a meeting and says ... 'Can't they find something else to talk about besides the Word of Wisdom; I am sick and tired of it'—of course he is, because he is full of stuff that the Word of Wisdom tells him to leave alone."[3]

From personal experience, President Grant knew that those who obey the Word of Wisdom will not be immune from all sickness and disease. He acknowledged that "being blessed does not mean that we shall always be spared all the disappointments and difficulties of life."[4] However, he repeatedly testified that when Latter-day Saints keep the Word of Wisdom, they receive blessings of health, prosperity, and spiritual strength that they would not be able to receive if they did not obey this law.

In the April 1933 general conference, President Grant said that because he had kept the Word of Wisdom, the Lord had allowed him to live to accomplish his mission on the earth. "I leave my testimony with you," he said, "that I believe as firmly as I believe anything in this world that I would not be standing here today talking to you if I had not obeyed the Word of Wisdom. When my appendix was removed it had broken, and blood poisoning, so they said, in the third and last stage, had set in. There were nine doctors present and eight said I had to die. The chief surgeon ... turned to President Joseph F. Smith, and said: 'Mr. Smith, you need not think of such a possibility or probability as that this man shall live. Why, if he should live it would be a miracle, and this is not the day of miracles.'

"That was the message delivered to me by Joseph F. Smith himself during his last sickness, and he said: 'Our doctor friend who said it would be a miracle has passed away. I never saw you looking healthier in my life than you do today, Heber.'

"I said to the nurse who told me regarding these nine doctors that I did not want to meet any of them, except the one who said and believed that I would pull through. She said: 'He is the house doctor; I will call him in.'

"I asked him why he disagreed with the others, and he smiled, ... and he said: 'Mister Grant, I just took a chance, sir. I have felt the pulse, sir, of thousands of patients, being a house doctor, in many, many hospitals, but I never felt a pulse just like yours, sir. Why, do you know, sir, in all of the tests that I made during an hour and three quarters that you were under the knife your heart never missed one single, solitary beat, and I made up my mind that that heart would pull you through.'

"What kind of a heart did I have? I had a heart that had pure blood in it, that was not contaminated by tea, coffee or liquor. That is why the poison in my system was overcome."[5]

"May God help you and me and every Latter-day Saint to observe the Word of Wisdom," President Grant once prayed, "that we may have health and hidden treasures of knowledge, and that God will allow us to live here upon the earth until we have filled out the measure of our creation."[6]

Teachings of Heber J. Grant

The Word of Wisdom is the law of life and health to the Latter-day Saints.

I find recorded in the Doctrine and Covenants a very short passage which reads:

"I the Lord am bound when ye do what I say; but when ye do not what I say, ye have no promise." [D&C 82:10.]

I wish that every Latter-day Saint would remember these few words. How I wish that they were engraven upon our memories and upon our hearts, and that we would determine that God shall be bound to fulfill His promises unto us, because we will keep His commandments. There is a law irrevocably decreed in heaven—so we are told by the Prophet Joseph—before the foundations of the world, upon which all blessings are predicated, and when we receive any blessing, it is by obedience to the law upon which it is predicated [see D&C 130:20–21]. If you and I desire the blessings of life, of health, of vigor of body and mind; if we desire the destroying angel to pass us by, as he did in the days of the children of Israel, we must obey the Word of Wisdom; then God is bound, and the blessing shall come to us.[7]

After telling us what is good for us [see D&C 89:10–17], the Lord makes a promise that is one of the most marvelous, one of the most uplifting and inspiring promises that could possibly be made to mortal man. He says:

"And all Saints who remember to keep and do these sayings, walking in obedience to the commandments, shall receive health in their navel and marrow to their bones;

"And shall find wisdom and great treasures of knowledge, even hidden treasures;

"And shall run and not be weary, and shall walk and not faint.

"And I, the Lord, give unto them a promise, that the destroying angel shall pass by them, as the children of Israel, and not slay them." [D&C 89:18–21.] ...

The Lord has told us through the Prophet Joseph Smith:

"If a person gains more knowledge and intelligence in this life, through his diligence and obedience than another, he will have so much the advantage in the world to come." [D&C 130:19.]

No man who breaks the Word of Wisdom can gain the same amount of knowledge and intelligence in this world as the man who obeys that law. I don't care who he is or where he comes from, his mind will not be as clear, and he cannot advance as far and as rapidly and retain his power as much as he would if he obeyed the Word of Wisdom.[8]

Another reason for which I am so anxious that the Latter-day Saints should observe the Word of Wisdom is that the Lord says it was given to us for our temporal salvation [see D&C 89:2]. I would like it known that if we as a people never used a particle of tea or coffee or of tobacco or of liquor, we would become one of the most wealthy people in the world. Why? Because we would have increased vigor of body, increased vigor of mind; we would grow spiritually; we would have a more direct line of communication with God, our Heavenly Father; we would be able to accomplish more. ...

Many a professed Latter-day Saint in hard times has lost the home that sheltered his wife and his children, who, if he had observed the Word of Wisdom, would have been able to save it. The violation of the Word of Wisdom has meant the difference between failure and success. By observing the Word of Wisdom, sufficient money to pay the interest on the mortgage would have been forthcoming, with additional help to take care of his family and farm.[9]

I do not want to interfere with any man's rights or privileges. I do not want to dictate to any man. But when the Lord gives a revelation and tells me what is for my financial benefit and the financial benefit of this people, because "of evils and designs which do and will exist in the hearts of conspiring men in the last days," [D&C 89:4] I do think that at least the Latter-day Saints should listen to what the Lord has said.[10]

No man or woman who is keeping the Word of Wisdom finds fault with it. Why? Because they know of the health they enjoy, they know of the peace, the joy, the comfort, the satisfaction that come to their hearts when they do what the Lord wants them to do.[11]

There is absolutely no benefit to any human being derived from breaking the Word of Wisdom, but there is everything for his benefit, morally, intellectually, physically and spiritually in obeying it.[12]

The law of life and health to the Latter-day Saints is to obey the Word of Wisdom.[13]

Those who disobey the Word of Wisdom are weakened physically and spiritually.

Do we ever stop to think that the Creator of heaven and earth, the Maker of all that we see in this great universe, the Father of our spirits, the Father of our Lord Jesus Christ in the spirit and in the flesh, has communicated with us, that he has given us counsel and advice such as will lead us back into his presence, that will give us vigor of body and of mind?

And yet there are hundreds, there are thousands among the Latter-day Saints to whom the Lord God Almighty has given a testimony and a knowledge that he lives, a knowledge that Jesus is the Christ, a knowledge that Joseph Smith was a prophet of the true and living God, and who are able to bear that witness and to testify of it at home and abroad, who, when the Lord God Almighty, the Creator of heaven and earth, tells them what is good for them, physically and spiritually, and writes them a letter, neglect to pay any attention to it. I am sorry to say that today there are many of the sons and daughters of the Latter-day Saints—some of the sons and daughters of leading men and women in this Church, who are having social gatherings and who think that it shows a spirit of liberality and of broadness to drink wine and to have their tea and coffee and to play their cards, and to do those things that we have been taught are not good for us. I am going to read to you a letter from the Lord to the Latter-day Saints. [After making this statement, President Grant read Doctrine and Covenants 89.][14]

The crying evil of the age is lack of virtue. There is but one standard of morality in the Church of Christ. We have been taught, thousands of us who have been reared in this Church from our childhood days, that second only to murder is the sin of losing our virtue; and I want to say to the fathers and to the mothers, and to the sons and daughters, in our Primary, in our Mutual Improvement Associations, in our seminaries and institutes, in Sunday School, in the Relief Society and in all of our Priesthood quorums—I want it understood that the use of liquor and tobacco is one of the chief means in the hands of the adversary whereby he is enabled to lead boys and girls from virtue.

Nearly always those who lose their virtue first partake of those things that excite passions within them or lower their resistance and becloud their minds. ... The young men and young women of today who think they are being smart by getting a little wine and a little liquor in their homes, and doing that which the Lord tells them not to do, are laying a foundation that will lead to their destruction eventually. They cannot go on breaking the commandments of the Lord without getting into the rapids. And what are the rapids? The rapids of moderate drinking [often] lead to excessive drinking, and excessive drinking leads to the destruction of body and of mind and of faith.[15]

When disease attacks a man whose body is full of tobacco and full of liquor, or who has been guilty of excesses and abuses in any phase of living, then he has no claim on these promises [referring to D&C 89:18–21].[16]

With the Lord's help, every Latter-day Saint can keep the Word of Wisdom.

The Lord has endowed me with no gift, with no power, with no ability, with no talent, but what he will ask me to give an account for it; and he has endowed every man, woman and child among the Latter-day Saints with the power and the ability to keep the Word of Wisdom.[17]

"A Word of Wisdom, for the benefit of the council of high priests, assembled in Kirtland, and the Church, and also the Saints in Zion—

"To be sent greeting; not by commandment or constraint—"

Some say, "Oh, that is how I get around it. It is not given by commandment or constraint." What is it? I will tell you what it is—

"but by revelation and the word of wisdom, showing forth the order and will of God." [D&C 89:1–2.]

When the Lord shows forth *his* order and *his* will, do not try to sing lullabies to your conscience, any one of you who is breaking the Word of Wisdom.[18]

One Sunday I attended a fast meeting in the morning, and another in the afternoon. One of the speakers at the latter meeting was Sister Anna Snow. …

She had come from Scandinavia and from her childhood had been addicted to the use of coffee, and thought she could hardly live without it. But finally, after reaching the age of eighty-two years, she was impressed that she had failed to do her duty in that regard and decided, on her eighty-third birthday, that she would keep the Word of Wisdom still more perfectly and stop drinking coffee. It nearly killed her, but she finally succeeded in overcoming the habit. And she stood up in humility before the people, confessing her failure at not having fully kept the Word of Wisdom and expressed her gratitude to the Lord for giving her the ability, even at this late date, to overcome her failing. And she testified to the benefit she had already received because of the improvement in her health by obeying this law of God.

I was profoundly impressed with her remarkable testimony. How I wish that every one of our good sisters, and our brethren as well, who, year after year, have gone on breaking this simple commandment of the Lord, could have been there and listened to her testimony.

I know a great many people have heard sermons on the Word of Wisdom for many years which have never made any impression upon them. I do not know how in the world we could make an impression upon some people. I know many individuals who have been labored with diligently in private, as well as by public teaching and admonition. But these labors have had no effect upon them. I feel in my heart that it is my duty to try to discover the weak points in my nature, and then pray to the Lord to help me overcome them. As I read the Word of Wisdom, I learn that it is adapted to the weakest of all the weak who are or can be called Saints [see D&C 89:3]. And I believe that it would be a wonderful aid in the advancement of the kingdom of God if all the Latter-day Saints would obey this simple commandment of the Lord. When I heard this aged sister testify that in her advanced years she had overcome, I wished that all Israel could have heard that testimony and been impressed by it.[19]

There is not a man or a woman among all the Latter-day

Saints but who could keep the Word of Wisdom if they got down on their knees ... and pray[ed] to God for help.[20]

Notes

1. In Conference Report, Apr. 1922, 165.

2. "Answering Tobacco's Challenge," *Improvement Era,* June 1931, 450.

3. In Conference Report, Apr. 1937, 13.

4. In Conference Report, Apr. 1945, 7.

5. In Conference Report, Apr. 1933, 10–11; spelling altered.

6. In Conference Report, Oct. 1927, 6.

7. In Conference Report, Apr. 1909, 109–10.

8. In Conference Report, Apr. 1925, 9–10.

9. "Safeguard," *Improvement Era,* Feb. 1941, 73; paragraphing altered.

10. In Conference Report, Oct. 1934, 129.

11. In Conference Report, Oct. 1937, 14.

12. In Conference Report, Oct. 1944, 8.

13. In Conference Report, Apr. 1926, 9.

14. In Conference Report, Oct. 1923, 8.

15. In Conference Report, Oct. 1944, 7–8; paragraphing altered.

16. "Safeguard," *Improvement Era,* Feb. 1941, 120.

17. In Brian H. Stuy, comp., *Collected Discourses Delivered by President Wilford Woodruff, His Two Counselors, the Twelve Apostles, and Others,* 5 vols. (1987–92), 5:60.

18. In Conference Report, Oct. 1937, 14.

19. *Gospel Standards,* comp. G. Homer Durham (1941), 284–85.

20. In *Collected Discourses,* 4:170.

Recommended and Other Reading

Students who desire to research the Word of Wisdom deeper should begin with Paul Peterson's 1972 M.A. thesis, "An Historical Analysis of the Word of Wisdom" (Brigham Young University), which has been reprinted by Benchmark Books, Salt Lake City (2005).

Paul Peterson and Ronald W. Walker collaborated on an excellent, prize-winning study titled, "Brigham Young's Word of Wisdom Legacy," *BYU Studies* 42:3–4 (2003): 29–64. Lester E. Bush provides a medical perspective on "The Word of Wisdom in Early Nineteenth-Century Perspective," *Dialogue* 14:3 (1981): 47–65. Thomas G. Alexander tells the story of Word of Wisdom reform in the tumultuous first decades of the twentieth century. See his *Mormonism in Transition* (Urbana: University of Illinois Press, 1996). A 1938 book that reflects President Heber J. Grant's emphasis is John A. and Leah D. Widtsoe, *The Word of Wisdom: A Modern Interpretation* (Salt Lake City, 1938).

To understand better the world in which the Word of Wisdom was revealed, nothing surpasses W.J. Rorabaugh's *The Alcoholic Republic: An American Tradition* (New York: Oxford University Press, 1979). On the tobacco conspiracy, see Richard Kluger's *Ashes to Ashes* (New York: Knopf, 1996), and Elizabeth M. Whelan's *A Smoking Gun: How the Tobacco Industry Gets Away with Murder* (Philadelphia: Stickley, 1984).

There is much information instantaneously available on the Internet. Use it cautiously. Precious little of it is written with the aim of providing sound knowledge based on scholarly research. Often the purveyors of such information are advocating some product or aspect of the Word of Wisdom. In such cases the Word of Wisdom is evoked to serve selfish interests, not the intent for which it was given.

Author's Biographical Information

Steven C. Harper is on the faculty in the Department of Church History and Doctrine at Brigham Young University and an editor of the Joseph Smith Papers. He earned a Ph.D. in early American history from Lehigh University. He is the author of a book on colonial Pennsylvania titled *Promised Land* and a short biography of Joseph Smith titled *Joseph the Seer*. He is married to Jennifer Sebring and they are the parents of Hannah, John, Abigail, Seth, and Thomas.

SETTING THE RECORD STRAIGHT SERIES

MORMONS & MASONS

GILBERT W. SCHARFFS, Ph.D.

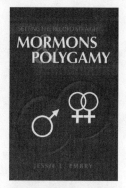

MORMONS POLYGAMY

JESSIE L. EMBRY

BLACKS THE MORMON PRIESTHOOD

MARCUS H. MARTINS, Ph.D.

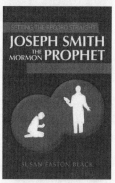

JOSEPH SMITH THE MORMON PROPHET

SUSAN EASTON BLACK

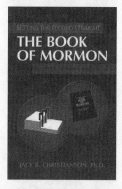

THE BOOK OF MORMON

JACK R. CHRISTIANSON, Ph.D.

EMMA SMITH: AN ELECT LADY

SUSAN EASTON BLACK

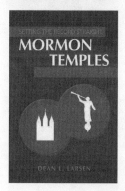

MORMON TEMPLES

DEAN L. LARSEN

THE WORD OF WISDOM

STEVEN C. HARPER, Ph.D.

JOSEPH SMITH: PRESIDENTIAL CANDIDATE

ARNOLD K. GARR, Ph.D.